IMAGINE!

Using Phantasy in Spiritual Direction
Marlene Halpin, Dominican

Religious Education Division
Wm. C. Brown Company Publishers
Dubuque, Iowa

About the Cover:

The mythological unicorn has variously been
depicted as the elusive power of the spirit, as healer,
as Christ-figure. On the cover of *Imagine That* the
unicorn is seen emerging from the sea (a
representation of the unconscious), graphically
conveying our hope that through the use of the
imaginative power of the spirit—phantasy—healing
and wholeness may ultimately prevail.

Illustrations and Design by Janet K. Conradi

Third Printing, 1984

Dedicated to: Mom and Pop
who enjoyed their own vivid imaginations and
who—unknown to us then—gave us the delight
of ours;

and to All of You
who, in using your own imaginations, may have
the fun of finding yourselves delightful.

Contents

Forward

I am delighted that Marlene Halpin has written this book. She has succeeded in capturing sound philosophical ideas in a refreshing approach to the use of our imagination and our emotions. The down–to–earth everyday manner of her presentation highlights rather than hides the sound philosophical principles upon which her thinking is based. No one will read this work without knowing more surely what imagination is, how to use it, and how to make it work to his or her advantage. Marlene introduces her readers to their own imaginations and helps us to know that imagination is a "simple, swift, and satisfying way to get at" deeper knowledge of ourselves.

Many people are divorced—or at very least, estranged— from aspects of themselves which are really the closest to them. All of us have at least a layman's acquaintance with the sciences of psychology and theology and with the arts of counseling and spiritual direction. That acquaintance has made many of us think that we dare not trust ourselves with matters of our personal and spiritual growth. Marlene invites us to rethink our attitudes and to look again at our feelings about our own resources for happiness and growth.

The individual phantasies are not presented to be "read through"; they are meant to be played with seriously. I have experienced Marlene's use of phantasy in a group setting. I know how much people have benefitted from those group experiences. I have listened to Marlene's care and concern and caution as she invited people to enter into their imaginations. That same respect, care, and concern are conveyed in these pages as she gives her readers advice on the use of the phantasies. It delights me that through the pages of this book people who cannot travel to one of her workshops will have access to this "phantastic" experience.

I believe this book is born of an awareness that many people are looking for more in life than they are getting from success, status, prestige, and wealth. Marlene directs her readers' attention to the existence and the possible uses of emotion and imagination in the everyday life of us all. And she shows us all concrete ways to recognize, understand, and make use of these human powers for our own personal and spiritual growth.

I appreciate just the clarity and conciseness of her descriptions of imagination, phantasy, emotions, and feelings. But Marlene has gone beyond clarity and conciseness; she shares with her readers a way to experience the benefit of using imagination and emotion—to come to know ourselves better and love ourselves more.

Marlene has consciously applied the use of imagination to the process of spiritual direction. For those people to whom spiritual direction is a concern—either because they are giving it or getting it—this book will be very useful. People involved in spiritual direction as director or directee often focus their attention on behavior and the motivation for behavior. The use of imagination, as Marlene describes it, will aid people in recognizing their behavior and motivation without requiring of them the soul–searching and often wrenching examination which is sometimes demanded. With an increased understanding of our behavior and our motivation will come a more relaxed recognition of the work of God in our lives.

I'm grateful to Marlene for her sharing of her own serious study, her devotion to people, her own vivid imagination and her interest in spiritual direction. I appreciate her sharing her dreams about individual spiritual direction in a group setting and her actual experience of doing spiritual direction in that way.

I suspect this book is one which individuals will share with their spiritual directors and which spiritual directors will share with those who seek them out for direction. It's the kind of book that can be used as a tool by an individual, by a group, or by a person and his or her spiritual director.

I'm glad Marlene Halpin, Dominican, wrote this book.

Keith Clark, Capuchin
St. Bonaventure Friary
Detroit, Michigan

Acknowledgments

IMAGINE THAT! came to be through the input and influence of a group of unusually dear people: Mrs. Lois George, whose enjoyment in typing (and retyping) the manuscript made writing the book even more fun; Mrs. Sandy Hirstein, whose editorial insights and suggestions made the work a delight; Fr. Jim Kerndt, who listened and encouraged this work from start to finish; Mr. Ernie Nedder, who envisioned the book after his experience with people using the phantasies; Dr. Donald J. Tyrell, who served as consultant for the first three chapters of the book and who taught me this use of phantasy; The Formation Class in Group Leadership at Aquinas Institute of Theology and Philosophy: Florine M. Bailey, Francine Barber, Angela Bugler, Ida Green, Dennis J. Kamalick, George E. Lyons, Daniel P. McLaughlin, Agnes B. Schelbert, and Julie Wiegard, who worked week by week with phantasies and responded with the beautiful integrity which is theirs.

Introduction

We're marvellously connected up on the inside. Everything about us has something to do with everything else. That's true physically. It's also true of us with respect to the way we know and what we want.

One of the things which diminishes our human living—as I see it—is that we tend to skip steps. That makes our living less complete, less consciously human, than it might be.

Some good people eat, drink, sleep, and take ordinary care of their health, but then skip over the "middle" part of being human and go right on to the intellectual or spiritual. Then— those of us who do this—wonder what's wrong with us, or feel guilty, because we don't feel good about doing good. Or being good. Often enough, I think, we don't allow ourselves to experience the great, rich mixture that human life is: the joy and the pain, the closeness and the loneliness, the interesting and the dull things, love and indifference, anger and sadness, the great and the ho hum, the exhilarating and those things that just have to be endured. It's all there. Real. Ready to be experienced, savored. Ready to come into awareness and fill out the crushed down areas of life.

The phantasy work explained in this book centers on the "middle" of the diagram: how we know, what attracts or repels us, on sense and emotional levels. Given that awareness, there follows the deep pleasure (sometimes, terror) of knowing ourselves better.

I've used these phantasies with men and women, adolescents and children, in a dozen or more states from New York to California. It always delights me how "of a piece" we are, in the myriad aspects of our living. What a wonderful integrity is ours—naturally.

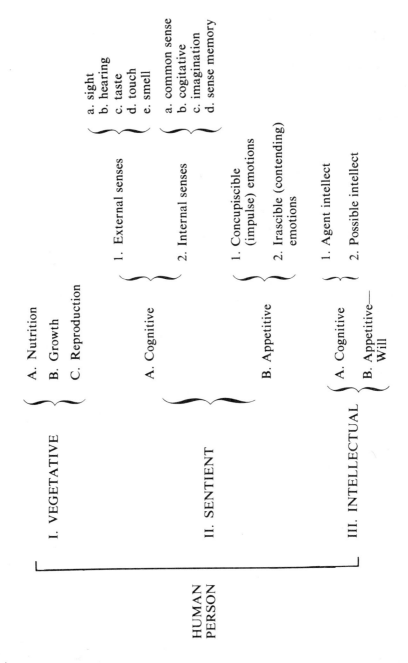

HUMAN PERSON

I. VEGETATIVE
- A. Nutrition
- B. Growth
- C. Reproduction

II. SENTIENT
- A. Cognitive
  1. External senses
     - a. sight
     - b. hearing
     - c. taste
     - d. touch
     - e. smell
  2. Internal senses
     - a. common sense
     - b. cogitative
     - c. imagination
     - d. sense memory
- B. Appetitive
  1. Concupiscible (impulse) emotions
  2. Irascible (contending) emotions

III. INTELLECTUAL
- A. Cognitive
  1. Agent intellect
  2. Possible intellect
- B. Appetitive—Will

Part I

IMAGINATION & PHANTASY

Imagination & Phantasy

People are startled when I ask, "What does imagination mean to you?" They respond with answers such as:
"Disney World."
"Kid stuff."
"Daydreams."
"A waste of time."
"I don't have any."
"Don't bother me with that nonsense."
"That's for artists, not for me."
A smile. Perhaps a knowing wink.

It surprises me somewhat to hear how reluctant many people are to acknowledge that imagination might play a real, useful, important part in their lives. For some the reluctance is a hangover from childhood scoldings, "Daydreaming, again! Now, what did I tell you?" "Stop daydreaming!" Popular custom treats imagination as though it were something bad—pleasurable, but frought with guilt feelings.

Yet in our everyday lives imagination is an efficient, practical, and reliable source of insight and productivity. There are many ways to use imagination. One of them is planning. All planning needs imagination. We plan our days, weekends, vacations. We plan menus and shopping lists. What to get Aunt Minnie for her birthday. How to get Pop to see a doctor. Christmas for the children. We plan ways to approach people: "What should I say?" . . . "How do I answer if he says this?" . . . "What if she turns me down?"

Another use of imagination is in anticipation of something pending. We live in delights of anticipation: a wedding, the birth of a child, a special occasion, meeting a loved one, seeing a good friend, making the last car payment; or in dread until we get the doctor's report, the result of the biopsy, the outcome of surgery. Why do some of us put off going to the dentist? How good are we in thinking a toothache out of existence? Or believing it will go away? Who among us will deny having a very active imagination when someone doesn't come home on time? As the clock's hands go around, and around again, so does our struggle between fear and anger. Do we call friends? The police? or "Just wait 'til he gets home!" If we really have no imagination, we would never begin to worry about what might have happened.

The fact is that our life is full of imagining. The pity is that we don't attend to it; and in not attending, we miss out on a lot of good things.

Perhaps our reluctance to admit the importance of imagination is rooted in the way we have been taught to think. Great emphasis has been placed on reasoning: proving, defending, making a case for something. *Linear* and *logical* are the words of the day. Now, logical thinking is a good thing. What I am suggesting is that it is not enough. The fact is, we cannot know without using imagination. Besides, logical thinking on its own is not powerful enough to regulate our behavior. Simply *knowing* what course of action is reasonable and appropriate in a certain situation will not necessarily result in our following that course of action. Living is not that simple. It's complicated by fear. I've been hurt in my life. So have you. Once we've been hurt, we respond in light of that hurt. "Once burned, twice shy," says folk wisdom. We get more protective of ourselves. "That's not going to happen to me again," I promise me. The trouble is, the more I keep people away from me so that I can't get hurt, the more do I keep myself from being hugged also.

People are apt to say: "Be reasonable!" Well, we should be. The fact is, we cannot truly be reasonable (saying, for instance, "If this, and if this, then that") unless first we are imaginative (receiving from senses and experience the "this" and the "this" and the "that" which the intellect knows and puts together). Centuries ago, St. Thomas noted that even the word "phantasy" (*phantasia*) gets its name from light (*phos*). Without light nothing can be seen. Without imagination (traces of sensations) nothing is seen (known). But imagination can go beyond this in allowing us to put things together in new and different ways. Sometimes we control it. For instance, in planning or in posing alternatives and imagining possible consequences. Sometimes we don't control it—as in dreams. Anyhow, while reasoning plays a role in why we do what we do, it is all of our life itself which teaches us how to survive. Children quickly find ways to say things which will please. Or, at least, keep them out of trouble. We adults can get around difficult situations by generalizing. We give answers which are no answers (but sound as if they might be) and which perhaps keep us from commitment, being quoted—or misquoted—or having information used against us. When standoffishness or noncommittal behavior becomes pattern, we tend to lose touch, even with ourselves.

The truth is that there are many factors that work against self–awareness. Life is not only busy, it is downright cluttered. Demands are unending and incessant. For every job that gets done, six more reproduce, multiplying faster than fruit flies.

When do we have time to sort out things? How can we better use our own resources? I suggest that we take a good look at one really marvellous, often underused, power with which we were all born: imagination.

Imagination is an internal sense. It's a treasure house of what the senses have experienced. We're used to talking about our external senses: sight, hearing, touch, taste, smell. When they don't function well we help them along with eyeglasses or hearing aids. Seeing, hearing, touching, tasting, and smelling are important to our living, and to our enjoyment of living.

These external senses put us in contact with both the outside world and our own bodies. Through the nervous system what the external senses receive is brought to the internal senses—senses located, for the most part, in the brain. (In the classical listing of the internal senses—imagination, common sense, sense memory, cogitative sense—all are in the brain. When new classifications and additions are made, there are additional locations. For instance, if balance is named an internal sense, the inner ear has to be identified as its location.)

It is in the brain that images are formed from sense data. Physiologists have traced different neural pathways for different imaginations: visual, auditory, somesthetic (including touch), motor, and olfactory. They all center in the more primitive part of the brain, then travel out to the cortex, and form a circuit back to their own particular brain center.

Imagination receives, retains, and manipulates sense impressions. These can come directly from experience, or may be from artificial signs (like words). Imagination is an inner sense of sight. Sometimes it is of one concrete thing (like picturing last year's Christmas tree when we finally got it decorated); sometimes it is a perception, in synthesized form (like, we can *know* in one perception, the condition of our house or room). Anything we have known or experienced can (with more or less effort) be sense–remembered and imagined, allowed to rest, or used for future planning. Imagination is truly a rich treasure house of our own living.

Common sense is basically a sense consciousness. It serves to make connections between sense data, between sense data and we who receive it. For instance, it lets us know that the apple we are holding and are seeing, and maybe the apple we are chomping, is the same object. It also lets us differentiate the apple from us, and lets us know that the apple serves our needs or desires.

Then there is sense memory which not only receives sense data (as do the other internal senses) but stores it and allows later recall and recognition. Neural pathways for the memory circuits also have been traced. They include visual, auditory, somesthetic, motor, and olfactory systems, as do the imagination circuits. Indeed, both memory and imagination circuits need to work closely together for healthy human functioning.

Finally, there is what in animals is known as instinct, and in humans as cogitative power. This "particular reason," or concrete reasoning, lets us know right away, on a sense level, that something is good or bad for us. It is beyond simple sensation. For example, suppose we are having soft–boiled eggs for breakfast. If, when the tops are cracked off, we get a very strong, unpleasant sulfureous smell, we do not go through a complicated abstract reasoning process as to whether to go ahead with that part of breakfast or not. Quicker than thinking we probably say "ugh" and relegate the noisome thing to the garbage.

All animals have senses, internal and external, more or less developed according to the animal. (There's a big difference between a clam and a horse.)

Imagination, working closely with sense memory, is the connector, the link between and among some of the dimensions of our human functioning. Imagination also influences how we handle the time dimension of our lives. Let's look at that briefly.

To suit our purposes, let's look first at imagination as it links our physical and emotional dimensions. Here imagination integrates the past with the present. Somebody passes by and you get a whiff of perfume. It might startle you into remembering Cousin JoAnn who always wore that scent. You smile, remembering what you bribed her to do by giving her a gift of that perfume. Or, you get a whiff of pipe tobacco that is the blend of which your dad was dearly fond. You smell it, and you see him lighting up contentedly after dinner. And you feel—however you feel about your dad. The radio plays "our song." Your heart is touched with the memories of when it became "our song," and of the subsequent history the relationship brought—deeper love, disappointment, anger, committed union, alienation. Always, though, it is "our song." Perhaps you walk into a strange house and the wallpaper in the bathroom puts you back into your grandmother's house. Memories of those visits come flooding back together with the feelings you had then. We could give many more examples, just as you probably could. The point is, in each instance, imagination is a dominant factor.

On level two, imagination works with our ability to think. Aristotle long ago said that as color is to seeing, so phantasm (the images the imagination makes) is to thinking. (Remember, imagination is a kind of internal sight.) Imagination helps us deal more effectively with both the present and the future. When we make plans or decisions— ordinary ones, such as what shall I wear today, or important ones, such as shall I take a new job offer—imagination helps us not only see what we want, but also foresee the consequences of our decisions. "If I buy a new car this year, I won't be able to meet the mortgage payments, and then. . . ." "If I make fun of the boss's wife and am overheard. . . ." "If I go ahead and do it without talking to the pastor first. . . ."

Imagination is a great help to us in making responsible choices. Of course—like any good thing—it can be abused. We all know people who are always imagining things— ourselves among them. I remember the first time I babysat for a neighbor. Never did a house creak so often or ominously. "Who's there?" I whispered a dozen times that night. Some people habitually imagine the worst. "Why is he late?" Some of us borrow trouble and here imagination serves us ill. Imagining, however, is a choice. We are perfectly capable of the kind of imagining which keeps us in fear, apprehension, and suspicion. We are equally capable of imagining what is productive, realistic, and beneficial to the quality of our life. Asking, "What if . . . ?" and running through a variety of possibilities (acceptable or not) opens the way to identifying more options which, in turn, can lead to freer and better decisions.

On another level, imagination connects the intellectual (our thinking process) with the spiritual (our valuing process) aspects of our living. All that we experience in our everyday living is changeable and changing. Still we long for permanency. Listen to love songs. How often do we hear words like: "always," "forever," "never leave me"? We want permanency when things are going well.

We expect, or at least hope for, stability. Sometimes we experience it, at least for a while. Then things change. Children grow up and leave home. Jobs terminate. Houses have to be sold. Friendships die. New friends bring new dimensions to our lives. So do new hobbies. Illness demands accommodations in living. Graduation flings us into the "real world." Births, divorces, deaths, remarriage begin the cycles over and over. Just when we seem to get settled, or get used to things, they change. Sometimes it's fun and exciting. Sometimes it's difficult and hard to let go of things or ways we are used to. It can be boring or it can be interesting, but changing it always is. We can *imagine* permanency. We can *imagine* stability. In a here and now way, that's not altogether possible in the real world. Of what use is it then?

Well, for one thing, imagining that we will be married until "death do us part"; or imagining that we shall be friends "forever" can be a real help. Most of us are experienced enough, I suspect, to know that those good things don't just happen. If you and I are to stay good friends, we need to work at it. If a marriage is to be lasting, it needs to be worked on. Not every six months, or every other year—but every day— with agreement and disagreement, with coming to know and reverence ourselves and each other as we go on living. With letting agreement and argument, sickness and health, pleasure and pain not divide us, but solidify the relationship. Even as I say "solidify" I mean deepen, strengthen, and always needing attention for more growth. So imagining "forever" helps us plan how to help make it happen.

For another thing, even though what we experience is impermanency, we can imagine a future permanency. How it will be, exactly what it will be like, is beyond precise knowing because it is beyond our experience. But it can be imagined. Imagination helps us bridge the gap between impermanency and stability, allowing us to deal with the present while positing a vision of the future. Some say that this use of imagination provides us with a psychological paradigm which allows us to affirm the notion of eternal life, of redemption and salvation, of heaven.

Making these connections from level to level: using imagination to connect what is happening to us and our emotions; imagining options and connecting possible consequences with them for good decision making; imagining what we want to be consistent in our lives (like a good marriage or friendship) and imagining what needs to be done to accomplish that; imagining a future life is something we all can do. And probably already do, more or less.

All these operations are quite ordinary, everyday occurrences. You might well be saying, "Yes, I experience those things. I see them happening in my own life." Yes, indeed. That imagination is, in fact, a very ordinary thing is an important point.

Diagrams of the brain which show those neural pathways of memory circuits and imagination circuits show them to be very, very close. In fact, they need each other to function. Our experience shows the same thing. Using memory and imagination we can replay just about anything we have ever experienced. "Remember when . . ." often starts a stream of consciousness that is in no way similar to remembering Lisa's new address or Dad's changed phone number. In "remembering when," we can simply recall and imagine past experiences or we can relive them emotionally. Sometimes we run through days or months or years of our lives without stopping to savor them. In imagination we can go back, enjoy, and bask in the love, the companionship, and the fun of them.

"Remember when" can also bring to mind trouble, hurt, and unfairness—the time someone gossiped, or downright lied, and we lost a friend, a place on a team or in a school play, an invitation, a job. Maybe we haven't let go of that injustice, and maybe it still gets in the way of our living well. What we choose to do with the memory is our decision.

"Remember when" may also be a link connecting how I feel or act NOW with something that happened THEN. I, for example, don't like bologna (harmless and bland as it is); I simply won't eat it. One day an elderly aunt was remembering the times we visited her family as children. How we loved to play with Sport, her dog! I remembered making him sit up for bologna skins. (We were not allowed to feed the dog the bologna, just the skins.) "Do you remember," my aunt asked, "how sick you got as a little girl, because you stuffed yourself with bologna to keep feeding the dog?" I remembered; I also remembered that night when I threw up into my bedroom slippers. I still don't like bologna. (Bedroom slippers are okay.) Remembering that doesn't make me like bologna any better, but it lets me know why I dislike it. That's a kind of trivial example. When the remembering and understanding have to do with more important things (like why I react to Laura so well or why I tend to avoid Vic), then I am in a position to make changes in my behavior.

There is something else to be said for imagination. In addition to the uses we have discussed to this point, there are still more ways to use this marvellous power.

Most of us are rather busy people. We go from one thing to another, "fitting in" necessary jobs as we go. When I was a child, that was not the way things were done. Mondays were laundry days at our house. It took all day to empty the hampers, sort clothes, wash them, blue the white things, hang the wet wash outside, chat with neighbors who were hanging out their laundry, too; stop for lunch, or a cup of tea with the neighbors; take the wash off the lines, fold, sprinkle and starch what needed to be ironed; iron and put clothes away. Those things smelled so good! How do I do laundry now? It goes into the machine when I'm on my way out; it goes into the dryer when I come back in (if I remember it). It's an "in–between" job, not a day's task liberally laced with living.

So our lives go. One thing is scarcely over before another starts. My contention is that as we pack in experiences, one on top of another, we find ourselves with no time to reflect upon, savor, or consciously integrate them with our living. They are consumed, like food swallowed whole. What those pieces of our living mean—how they are influencing our attitudes, behavior, self–image, and perception of others—is available to us, but it goes unattended.

Occasionally, something or someone nudges us to awareness. When we're lucky enough for someone to say, "Well, have you looked at it this way?" . . . "Do you know that . . . ," we might well respond, "I never thought of it that way. Thanks! It makes a difference."

Still, there's a good deal of our experience which is very tightly packed in and away, down deep inside. Some of it is perhaps labeled, "no time"; "not important"; "it hurts too much." "It hurts too much" is often a real bugaboo for us. So instead of dealing directly with my hurt, I eat too much, I work too much, I sleep too much, I drink too much. As I keep going, "it hurts too much" is ignored; it becomes a walled up lump somewhere in my middle. Eventually "it hurts too much" turns into, "I'm not good enough," "I don't count," "They don't care," "I don't care," "I'm sick." Maybe I don't say the words aloud, but my actions ultimately shout them. My attitudes change subtly, perhaps without my noticing. I change. Time after time I am hurt and bewildered by what people say about me because "I'm not like that." They don't understand what I really feel. Maybe they don't. Maybe I don't.

That is the dismal side of confronting what is within us. There's also an enjoyable, fulfilling side. It has to do with knowing and loving ourselves, other people. Imagination helps with that part of living, too.

Socrates, the granddaddy of Western philosophers (a man who spoke his mind plainly, if ever one did), said: "Know yourself. All widom lies there."

Both the Hebrew and Christian Scriptures command us to love the Lord our God with all our heart, and with all our soul, and with all our mind. Then we are commanded to love our neighbor *as* ourselves.

As ourselves. Not *more* than ourselves because that is impossible. We are no help to others if we are not appropriately attentive to ourselves. Commercial airlines are very aware of that. (Listen to the flight attendant telling "those travelling with small children" to adjust, if needed, the oxygen mask on themselves first, then on the small child.)

Before I can *love* anyone, I have to *know* the person. That's just plain common sense. Suppose you come into my room and see something on my desk. Well, you could see it is purple. It smells a bit musty. You poke it gingerly and it squashes, so you know it's soft. Would you want it? Would you be likely to say, "Wow! What a find! I'm going right out and buy myself one." Or would you be more likely to ask, "What is that?" Followed probably by: "What on earth is it for?" THEN, and only then, would you know if you'd want one or not—if you'd be willing to invest in one or not. We cannot like, want, love something we don't know. That's true of things. It's true of people. Knowing comes first. Then loving (or not).

So, of course, that includes knowing me—not just my inadequacies and failures, but also the good things within my human limits. I cannot be everything to everybody—no more than can food, clothing, or shelter satisfy all human needs.

You and I are each someone unique. We are literally different from everyone else in this world. We are human and share the kind of being we are. We have other things in common with many other people: nationality, religion, race, sex. Still, each of us is unique. No one has my exact history, my exact experiences, actions, and reactions. There's not another person in this world who has my network of relations, friends, acquaintances, and not–so–much–liked people. And every one of us, made by God with infinite prodigality, is "very good," as the first book of the Bible says. It's important I come to know myself, my goodness. To love myself. To acknowledge in me the goodness of God's creation. Then I am able to know others, to acknowledge the goodness of God's creation in others, to love others.

Self–knowledge is an ongoing task. I come to know myself through my own experiences and my reflection on them. Your feedback helps a good deal. We have already considered how busy our lives are, and how much living gets squashed in and unattended. Because of that, and because of some of our fears and denials, I'm going to add another way to know ourselves. Imagination.

Suppose someone were to ask me: "How do you feel about yourself? How are you relating to Dorothy? To Mom? To Joe? How important is God to you in your life?" Or, suppose the questions were to go this way: "What do you expect from life? How do you act when you are confused? Uncertain? Challenged? Do you understand why you act that way? Do you deal with it when you understand?"

Many times people, if they don't give easy or flippant answers ("I feel great about myself." "I relate fine." "Of course God is important, what do you think I am anyway?") can go on and on and on. Confusion, explanations, excuses, rationalizations can be almost endless. Perhaps I don't want to face what is inside me. Possibly I find it too complicated to explain. Maybe I am confused. Or maybe stalling, avoiding, and denying are my ways of coping.

For myself, and for the people who invite me into their lives, I find that imagination is a simple, swift, and satisfying way to get at those sorts of things. In my experience I have found that imagery helps me know myself in some aspects with more clarity. Using imagination for this kind of phantasizing is different again from using phantasy as a means of stress reduction, or in positive thinking, or healing of memories. It is for *knowing* myself and my concerns better. With such recognition I am freer to make better decisions for my life. With this knowledge I find myself saying, "Yes, that is so." With that insight, there oftentimes comes a deep relaxation, peace in body and mind. I like it.

The phantasies proposed in this book are for these purposes: to enable us to know ourselves better; to enable us to love ourselves more truthfully; to enable us to love our neighbor as ourselves; to enable us to expand the use of our capacities for knowing and loving. With knowledge and love less encumbered by ignorance, indifference, and unacknowledged emotions, I am capable of making better decisions. "And just what do you mean by better, more mature decisions?" you might be asking. For me that means keeping the basic rule for moral human decisions: "All things considered, do the best thing possible under the circumstances." That's pretty much the way St. Thomas defines prudence. He also says that there is no moral virtue without prudence being part of it. "All things considered, do the best thing possible." The decision might be mistaken. It won't be sinful. What knowing and loving do better is enlarge the "all things considered." I hope that more mature decisions, and more fulfilled living will be the result of using these phantasies.

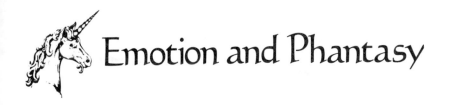# Emotion and Phantasy

You will notice after you've entered into the phantasy section of this book that I never ask the question, "What do you think?" My questions generally are expressed as, "How do you feel?" In asking for such a response, technically I'm not being precise. Were you to answer with technical precision, you'd be restricted to things like: "I feel cold" or "thirsty" or "in pain" or "very well" or "hungry." *Feeling* in itself is restricted to physical sensation or mental state. But in our more ordinary, everyday speech, *feeling* is commonly interchanged with *emotion,* and emotions have a very large repertoire. And it's uncovering emotion that we're aiming for as a beginning point in the phantasies.

Why? Well, for one thing, I think emotions can be among our best teachers. Unfortunately, I also think that a good number of us have suffered from poor teaching about emotions. If we have internalized poor teachings, or if we abide by the rules of their mistaken notions, then our lives may be emotionally deprived. I say that with certainty because emotions are an integral part of our being human and, therefore, play an important role in our lives.

For those among us who are Roman Catholic and old enough to have studied (memorized) the Baltimore Catechism, to the question: "What is man?" we replied, "Man is a creature composed of body and soul, and made to the image and likeness of God." Another question's answer told us, "This likeness is chiefly in the soul." Now, those are two questions and answers with which I have no post–Vatican II difficulty (except that I'd want to change "man" to "human being"). My problem with the phrasing is not rooted in what is *said,* but with what is left out. (In a way it's like discussing sin: commission is bad, but so—and sometimes worse—are sins of omission.)

15

"Well," you might be asking, "what's left out?" I'll answer with a question: " 'Creature made of body and soul,' and 'made to the image and likeness of God . . .' Where's the link? The connection? How do we know from experience that body and soul are a unity?" That's no easy question. Down the centuries and long before the birth of Jesus, philosophers have struggled with that same question and come up with a variety of answers. (Remember, psychology, as a science separate from philosophy, is only a tad more than one century old.)

For those among us who hold "composed of body *and* soul" to mean that we are one person (not, for instance, that we are all soul and put on a body like a coat; or—at the other end of the spectrum—that we are just the classiest of animals), one way of demonstrating the truly deep unity of body and soul is by emotional experience.

Suppose you were walking down the street one day. Just in front of you is a young woman pushing a baby stroller. In it a very young child is sitting up and waving a toy. You are approaching a corner. Suddenly a truck comes around the corner, misses a signal, and crashes into another truck. With the collision one truck bursts into flames. To your horror, the driver tries to get out of the cab. Just as he starts through the open window, another sheet of flames engulfs him and with a scream he falls back inside and disappears into the flames.

You, the young woman, and the baby saw and heard the same things. What's the baby doing? Having been startled by the noise and fire, the baby is probably crying. How about you? Are you surprised, horrified, helpless, sick, pitying, or perhaps running for help? What's the difference between you and the baby? You *understand* what's happening. Beyond tortured metal and fire, beyond sound, sight and heat, you understand that a man's being burned to death. And you can't do a thing about it.

Now, that's pretty upsetting for you. But suppose the young woman who was walking ahead of you recognized the truck driver. Suppose he were her husband. Her emotional reaction would be far more intense than yours, for her personal involvement is greater than yours, and yours is greater than the baby's.

Emotions involve physical responses, such as, rapid heart beat, weak knees, cold feet, dry mouth, sweaty palms or arm pits, twitching, queasy stomach. The body always responds. Immediately there is some response, a result of choice, to the emotion. To express it we might choose to cry, laugh, dance, run away. We might decide to embrace, avoid, sing, waste away, give up, be determined. Without emotions life would be like a snowy black and white T.V.—no color, with even the black greyed.

Besides adding color to life and letting us know we are alive, emotions are fine teachers. Since emotions involve both body and spirit, sometimes they alert us to things of which we're not yet conscious. For instance, suppose you and I were standing face to face, conversing. A man comes along and steps on my foot. It hurts. I'm feeling the pain in my foot and I am irritated. Perhaps I am irritated enough to start saying: "You stupid idiot! Why don't you look where you're going!" Maybe I get as far as "You stu . . ." when I see the man is wearing dark glasses and holding a white cane.

The incident remains the same—my foot was stepped on and hurts. Different emotions. "I'm sorry. Had I seen you coming I'd have called out, or moved." I feel pity, compassion, empathy. I don't want to be visually handicapped and I feel sorry for anyone who has that burden.

Then I discover he's a fraud! He's not blind at all, but a charlatan who has found a lucrative corner where his begging is amply rewarded.

The external circumstances are the same: my foot has been stepped on and hurts. But now I feel anger, resentment, and vengeance. I think it's despicable to imitate a blind person like that! I really get on my high horse!

What makes the difference in my reactions? I've gone from annoyance to irritation; to compassion, pity, and empathy; to anger, resentment, and vengeance—all due to the same physical event.

Do a slow replay of the emotional changes. What was the assumption, the judgment which preceded each emotion? You see, every emotion is preceded by a prior judgment. It's not a judgment consciously alluded to, perhaps. Generally it's made much too quickly for that. But it is there.

In the first instance, I was irritated. My prior judgment was that people should look where they're going (then my foot wouldn't have been stepped on). Is that a reasonable judgment? Ordinarily, yes. I won't work on changing it. In the second case my prior judgment was, "He couldn't help it. He's blind. I wouldn't want to be blind." Hence the sympathy, the compassion. I don't want to change that judgment either. My third assumption was built on my belief that "it's wrong to pretend to be handicapped for financial gain." (And he should have been careful not to step on me.) I think that judgment is reasonable, too, so I won't change any behavior over it.

Once, after attending a meeting with friends, one man told me that he was so irritated he thought he'd best excuse himself from dinner and the movie we had planned. I told him that I was disappointed, but that his decision was fine with me. Then I thought again. "Do you want to leave it at that, or would you rather work it through?" He opted for the latter.

We examined his irritation and anger and found when it took place. Three men had been heckling a speaker who is a friend. It wasn't just the heckling, however, that bothered my friend. He saw the heckling as a demand for attention in an area that was not the immediate concern of the speaker nor of the professional organization in which context it took place. "That's it!" said my colleague, "Those three are new to this organization and don't realize how out of place their sort of questioning was." He made two decisions. One was to speak to the three gentlemen involved about the purpose of the meeting. The other was to go to dinner and a movie, which he did in good spirits.

Basic philosophy teaches that there is no effect without some cause. Things, in truth, never "just happen." There is always a cause, just as there's always a cause for emotion, and that is a prior judgment called into play by whatever the immediate situation is. I find it very helpful, both for myself and others, to freeze the emotional moment and walk slowly backwards to just before it happened.

Suppose my colleague in the last example had not attended

to his bad humor and had gone to dinner with the rest of us? Certainly his enjoyment would have been diminished. Probably ours, in his company, would have been less. That's a good reason to attend to emotions.

Another reason to attend to emotion is in order to understand motivation. There is no motivation without emotion. Any human action I consciously perform (that's different from the automatic ones, such as breathing or digesting) I perform because I want to. Or, foreseeing consequences, I'd choose to do it rather than suffer what would happen if I didn't. I still choose to do it.

The belief or judgment that motivates an emotion may be conscious or not. If it is unconscious, I did consciously make it at some time, in some way, during my life. When something happens which impacts me either as good for me, and I want it, or as bad for me, and I want to avoid it, naturally I react. But before I act, I make a decision.

That is a very important fact to pay attention to. As a child I had been taught that anger is a sin. I was taught, too, that I should be careful in the company of men because they can have a strong impact on me and that might be a sin for me. This sort of teaching is what I referred to earlier. I think it is poor teaching because it skips a step—a crucial step. When something happens which I perceive as unfair, my immediate, normal reaction is anger. That does not mean that I shall do something sinful out of the anger. It's an insult to me and it's an insult to the freedom which God gave me, to make that assumption. Between my anger and my action, there is decision. Feeling my anger is no more good or bad than feeling my pulse. What I decide to do about my anger, or because of it, is good or evil. And no matter what I decide to do, I need to discharge the energy my body has been charged with from the anger. To discharge energy appropriately is a very good thing. It's good for my body: it prevents ulcers, headaches, and tension. It's good for my relationships: it keeps them clear and current. Anger is not a sin. What I decide to do in light of my anger may be virtuous or it may be sinful. Having sexual feelings about another person is not a sin. If anything, it shows that I am alive and well. What I decide to do about those feelings is good or sinful.

Ignoring or denying emotion is simply not helpful for healthy living on physical or emotional levels. It really doesn't work to say, "I'll let myself feel affectionate (toward members of my sex and little children only); and sad at other's misfortunes (not if they deserved them, of course); and hope for heaven; and be glad when I succeed at something (but not too glad, because then I'll be getting into pride). I won't let myself feel sexually attracted to anyone except my spouse (and even then . . .); or jealous (nice people don't); or despairing (my faith is too strong for that); or hateful toward anyone (because I'm a good Christian and Christians don't hate).

It really doesn't work. Why not? Well, suppose you have a brand new car. The engine has all brand new parts on the brand new engine block. And it all works well. So you say, "I'll take out a few spark plugs, and maybe one belt, and siphon out the brake fluid. That's only three things." What expectations would you have of that car's ability to perform?

Well, what expectations have you of your ability to perform as a human being when you don't allow yourself attraction, jealousy, despair, and hate? When one emotion is shut down, all suffer. There's not much mileage in that. When some emotions are shut down, all are necessarily affected by the shutdown. It's like the car engine. Even if I take out only a few spark plugs, and don't bother with a belt or the brake fluid, that fine new car will not go. It's not quite that drastic with us human beings. We'll "go," but not well. We are made a whole person, one, all connected inside. With emotional shutdown (even only one emotion) our behavior is affected. Adversely. Decision making is impoverished. Motives become spotty and brown around the edges. And what does it say to God? "Some of the ways you gave me to operate aren't very nice, so I don't want them."

That response is a trap. Unless we are very holy and very simple (I think they are close together), it's a trap we fall into easily.

If I don't describe what I mean by "jealousy" or "anger" or "vanity" or "needing to be in control," I can keep those emotions "out there" as some sort of abstract category. Nice people aren't angry, jealous, vain, or powerhungry. I'm a nice person. Therefore, I am not angry, jealous, vain, or powerhungry. True? Maybe it is. Probably it is not. Do I repress emotion consciously? Maybe not. Do I do it intentionally? Of course. I hide it; I don't look at it; I refuse myself permission to see those parts of me. By doing this I have already disallowed myself the privilege of seeing myself wholly, of knowing myself well, of loving myself appropriately. It's a self–defeating way to live, and a very common one. St. Paul put it well in Rom. 7:14–23 when he wrote of doing the things we don't wish to do, and not doing those we do wish to do. He struggled with the paradox. I know no one who doesn't.

There are some good side effects to emotional honesty. Confusion in life diminishes. For instance, consider confusion. Confusion is real when there is inadequate information, or conflicting data. Often in the course of human living confusion is self–induced. Frequently it means: "I'm too honest to lie; I'm not honest enough to say the truth." What I label me, then, is "confused." With emotional honesty whining will also decrease. Whining is a great way to get around being angry, especially if you are a nice person. Furthermore, I'll be more likely to mean it when I ask for advice and not be surreptiously angling for approval. I'll be far more likely to be open with people. In the past, when I have said openly what I felt or thought about something, I've been hurt by ridicule or by the information being misused. Probably I'll be hurt again, because I'd rather be open (not naively, if I can help it!) than not. If I were to give in to the urge to protect myself I'd be hurt less. Protecting myself keeps people out: hurting ones, and also loving ones. When I put up defenses no one gets in: foe or friend. I'll be less loved. Consequently, I'll be less loving. I think that's a selfish and sad way to go about living.

Why do we act this way? To avoid pain? I suppose so. I think it's a sad thing to see people living their lives with a high priority on avoiding pain. I don't like pain. I don't know many people who do. But I refuse to give my best energy to avoiding it. There are more important things to be doing as I spend my life. Besides, I've learned that while being open may bring more hurt, it affords less damage. Hurts can repair well, and usually without too much difficulty. Damage (for instance, being love–famished from keeping people out) is a much more serious affliction. Moreover, I like being alive and being aware of the many facets of my living.

So much for the poor teaching which says that anger is a sin; or that emotions are unimportant and insignificant.

Now let's look at the array of emotions we have. Then we can spend a little time talking about attending to them.

Emotions have been classified and categorized in a number of ways. I like to deal with them in terms of when they occur: ordinarily, as part of everyday living; or extraordinarily, at times of special significance. In both kinds, there can be an attraction toward something we perceive as good for us, or a rejection, a tendency away from something seen as harmful. Among the ordinary emotions are liking, wanting, enjoying; or disliking, avoiding, sadness.

Let's start with the emotions we ordinarily experience. If I see something as beneficial, as good for me—whether it is present or absent—I will love or like it. If it isn't present, I want it. If it is present, and I have it, I delight in it; I enjoy it. Think of something you've wanted, something expensive, like a new car; or something useful, like a new washing machine. You've seen a model you like. All the features (you want) are there. You like it. Before you own it, you want it. When you take possession, you experience delight, joy. If you don't get it, you are disappointed.

On the other hand, suppose you see something as harmful for you. Whether it is presently there or not, you hate or dislike it (depending on how seriously you see yourself able to be harmed). You direct your efforts to avoiding it. If it is present, you feel regret and sadness. When I have to work with someone who is very sarcastic, I don't enjoy my work time. I dislike being made fun of. It's worse when the person is really witty and others laugh. Whether that other person is present or not, I dislike the sarcastic person. I feel aversion and recoil when that one comes into the room, and I feel sorry for myself when I can't avoid mutual presence.

Is there anything extraordinary in what I just said? I don't think so. Then should we not feel free to acknowledge that we love, like, want, desire, delight in, and enjoy some things while we hate, dislike, feel aversion to, recoil from, and are sad over other things? Is any one of them less real than any other? I think not. Do all these emotions come into my life? I think so. Saying (or having said about us), "I don't like her," is not a value judgment that we (or they) are evil people. It simply gives expression to the fact that there is not an attraction at that time, to that person. What's so difficult about that? For either of us? Do you like every kind of food you encounter? Architecture? Music? If you don't like a particular kind, does that make it unworthy or evil? Of course not.

When somebody says to me, "I don't like you," I don't particularly jump for joy and feel all warm and fuzzy inside. "Well, I don't like you, either!" I perhaps respond. It might be true that I don't. I might also be getting even in a hurry and protecting myself. Whatever the response is, let's go back to the moment of, "I don't like you."

Am I embarrassed, especially if someone else is there? I suppose I am. Am I hurt? Probably. Am I relieved it's out in the open? Maybe so. Now do what we did before: freeze the moment of embarrassment or hurt. What is the prior judgment upon which my emotional reaction is based? Is it, "Everybody should like me." What's implicit in that statement? "I'm so marvellous, so good, so universally appealing that every personality type in the world has to like me." Do you really believe that? Is it possible that someone might prefer a personality type other than yours? If so, why are you hurt? Unlike my response to the man who stepped on my foot (and I still think people should look where they are going), which called for no behavior change on my part, in this instance I might want to change the way I habitually react to such a situation. How? Again, look at the assumption: I am so good everybody has to like me. But this person doesn't. I still may not like it, but by attending to the judgment I need not let the situation upset me so much. I can learn to accept it and move on tranquilly.

"Oh," you might be saying, "but I like that person." Then

it's a hard pronouncement to accept. However, there's not real friendship without mutuality. Or, you might be saying, "It's important to me for that person to like me." Maybe. Perhaps your job depends on it or admission to a club. Or there may be a further question to be considered. Will that person evaluate you, recommend you, fairly? Would you? I think most of us would be fair. We don't have to like someone to say, "He's a good manager"; "You can depend on her; she's a very responsible person." If we can be fair, won't we also give the other person credit for similar honesty? (Unless, of course, experience with that person says, "not so.") In work situations we have to work with people. We're not paid to like them, or they us. Liking or not liking is neither good nor bad in the moral sense. Both are ordinary human emotions. Between the emotional impact, however, and action, there is a decision. (Does that sound familiar?) The behavior which results from that decision is what can be judged good or bad. Decisions are better made, that is, with more truthfulness and freedom, when we are consciously aware of our emotions and the judgments which precede, cause, and are part of them.

Let's go back to the other kind of basic emotions—the ones which occur at times of special significance. Hope, courage, fear, despair, anger are emotions present at very difficult times. As with all emotions, these are attracted to what is perceived as beneficial to me and repelled from those people or things which I perceive as harmful to me. These operate if the good we want to obtain, or the evil we want to avoid, is very difficult to secure or elude. If it is something I want very much, but it is very difficult to get, yet I judge it attainable, I have hope. If I want it very much, but it is very difficult to get, and I judge it to be beyond my obtaining, I despair. Both of these reactions are generated by something I perceive as beneficial to me.

On the other hand, those things which I perceive as harmful to me will generate other emotions. If it is an injurious situation I believe I can overcome, then I need to be brave, courageous, perhaps daring. If the threat of hurt is present and unfair to me, I may get angry or desperate. Fear comes when I want very much to avoid something I see as hurtful to me. If the threat of hurt is present, dejection may result.

Let's consider some specific examples. Suppose I am twenty–two years old, a straight "A" student, and have been accepted by a good medical school. I can very reasonably hope to become a physician, and then a specialist. There are difficult, long years of study ahead, but the goal is attainable. Suppose, however, I am forty–eight years old and very much in love with a young person, who comes to work one day in great excitement: "I'm so happy! I got engaged last night!" I could well be hopeless, despairing of marriage with this person. I see my goal as unattainable.

Daring, bravery, and courage are needed at special times. Were I to see a baby crawling near the edge of a dock, it would take no special courage on my part to block the baby's path or to set the child down in a safer place. Were I to see a crawling baby come near the edge of a dock, and a fire breaking out between the child and me, it would take definite physical courage to protect the child. Other actions require moral courage. Might not that be said about a person returning to school at thirty or forty or fifty? Or about people who change careers in their forties or fifties? What about people who take a stance for social justice? In many circles that is not a popular thing to do. What about those who put themselves on the line, ministering to "those people," whatever "those people" mean under the circumstances? What about people who demonstrate for a cause—not because it's the thing to do, but from a deep moral conviction?

I remember the first time someone I knew marched for a cause. It was right after Vatican II. Sisters were very much inside convents. I remember being very touched when this Sister said, at a community meeting, why she had to do it. With several others she had been working with the poorest people in a slum area of New York City—working with the people and with the landlords as well as county officials. After months and months of negotiations, the landlords had promised to make improvements in the tenement houses. Stairs would be replaced; wires would be put back into walls; holes filled with plaster; plumbing repaired; a rodent exterminator sent in. When all was ready to go, the landlords banded together and reneged on all promises. "How could I not stand with my people?" asked the Sister. With tears, she told how afraid she was—how distasteful it was to her. For her, worst of all, was the scorn and derision of the policemen along the route of march. Her dad and brothers were police officers. She grew up with police friends in her home. Sister evidenced another thing—an array of contending emotions. Brave she was; scared, too; loving the people; angry at the landlords; finding her public stance repugnant; afraid of the police along the way, of her family's reaction; of how the community would respond; hopeful that the protest would turn out well, but not sure. There's hardly a time when only one emotion is at play. It's a good thing to pay attention to the total bundle that an emotional experience is.

Psychologists have known for a long time we don't have one single emotion for long. Recent research shows that there is a five- or ten-second limit on undiluted emotion—there's such a rapid succession of them. Dismay, surprise, disgust, pity, helplessness can succeed each other in seconds. We experience the whole bundle. In our own lives it's realistic to be aware of the various strands in order to deal with the situation more appropriately.

What would be the good of it had Sister said of her public protest, "Oh, it was nothing"? It was *not* nothing. For a woman like her it was a great deal. She shared her feeling as she experienced it. That was the beginning of my community's public policy of supporting our sisters in their public stances on social justice issues. One woman's emotional honesty served her well. It continues to serve others with support.

Is it wrong, weak, ungrownup to be afraid? I guess it depends a lot on what we're afraid of, and why. Fear sometimes helps me make good choices. I'm afraid to drive after having a drink. Therefore, I don't. I'd be afraid to fall off the roof of a high building. I'd be very afraid of a hostile person holding a knife at my throat or pointing a gun at me. There's no question: I judge these acts dangerous to my well-being, and do my best to avoid them. Other kinds of fears bear examination. Am I fearful that not everyone will like me? Wallowing in that fear is counterproductive. Examine the assumption behind it. To hold on to that assumption displays some arrogance. Arrogance flows from a false self–image: a "poor me" or a "grandiose me." The kind of insecurity it evidences says: "I'm not good enough." What's the assumption behind that? Is it, "I must be perfect"? Sometimes I see that assumption as a violation of the first commandment. There is *one* God. I am a creature; by nature I am imperfect. That I am *is* good enough.

Am I fearful that I'll fail? I might. It might be unpleasant. Does the fear prevent my trying? I hope not. What's the assumption behind that kind of incapacitating fear? "I must succeed. Always." Always! How dull! How unreal! (What about the first commandment?) I think it was Edison who, when asked to comment upon so many, many unsuccessful experiments, replied: "I didn't fail 10,000 times. I merely found 10,000 things that didn't work." If we are so afraid of failing, we might also need to look at why we are afraid of succeeding. What reward to we get from letting the fear of failure immobilize us? What price do we pay for keeping that fear alive?

In summary, then, we can talk about emotions as part of our human being. They are action tendencies toward things we judge as good for us, which contribute to our well–being, or away from things appraised as harmful to us. Emotions produce physiological changes. Our body shares the appraisal and expectation of what will happen or is presently happening (as when someone dearly loved unexpectedly enters the room, or when we open the door to our room and find an utter stranger there).

Emotional stability is not synonymous with ignoring or hiding memories, impulses, behaviors of which I am not proud. Stable people aren't unfeeling, unresponsive. I'd suggest that they are stable precisely because they are aware of what is happening, how they are responding, and because the freedom that is the result of emotional truthfulness allows them to live well, according to their own decisions. Our lives are full of highs and lows, lights and darks, intimacies and separations, hurts and pleasures, injustices and acknowledgments, tears and laughter, pain and delight, interest and boredom, satisfactions and disappointments. Why not be aware of and experience them for what they are? Why not incorporate them into the fabric of our lives? Why not live with their richness at our disposal?

Imagination and emotions are related. They are part of our very human being. They are designed to contribute to our awareness of experience: both pleasing and displeasing, pleasurable and painful, satisfying and harmful. Not only do they provide consciousness of the moment's interaction or event, they contribute to our decision making.

Emotions push imagination. There seems to be a sort of internal itch in each of us to make sense of things. Almost as soon as children can speak, is not "why" one of their favorite words? Adults, too, ask "why." "Why am I treated this way?" "Why don't my friendships last?" "Why don't things turn out better for me? I do try so hard!"

The phantasies which follow are designed to surface our emotional attitudes. Attitudes are the result of repeated experiences and have become habitual ways in which we respond. Often enough, phantasies indicate how we deal with life's experiences, such as obstacles, authority, relationships. They may evidence how we look at ourselves when our attitudes become clear to us. On the evidence of our own internal resources, we are in a position to look at our lives more realistically. Following from this we are better able to say, "I see that I do that," and decide, "and I'll continue it." Or, "I don't like it; I'll change my behavior." Motivation to change is most likely to succeed when it comes from within us (as opposed to some threat from the outside).

Being consciously present to our emotions, trusting imagination to provide us with phantasies, I think, is a very useful human experience. I hope you find it worthwhile for your life.

Using the Phantasies

Before presenting some phantasies, I'd like to mention a few practical points.

Rule #1. Phantasies are not logical. They do not follow the laws of syllogistic reasoning. Content or outcome are not plotted, planned, thought out, nor need they be defended. (The direction they take, the purpose of each one, is known and deliberately chosen.) There is no such thing as a "wrong" or "bad" phantasy. Images may be pleasant, bizarre, startling. Images which emerge indicate aspects of ourselves or of our situation, and our emotional attitude toward them. These images are neither "good" nor "bad." What makes them "good" or "bad," "right" or "wrong," is what we decide to do—our behavior. Phantasies, then, are something like invited guests at our threshold. We open the door and they present themselves. They can be very good teachers if we permit them to serve us that way.

Phantasies are not mere replays of former situations. Nor are they minidramas thought out, edited, and performed. We have the power to do that but then they are not phantasies in the real sense; they are plain memory or daydreaming. Memory and daydreaming have different effects from these phantasies.

If we choose to let go (that is, physiologically speaking, if we suppress the cerebral cortex—the part of the brain which thinks, organizes, selects, censors), if we choose to *not–think*, phantasms will emerge. They will come because they are natural expressions always available to us, if we but permit ourselves to attend to them.

Once we give simple attention to the phantasies (letting go of the comfort found in more customary thinking and criticizing and of attempts to "make it come out good") they will freely emerge and be both good friends and teachers. The important thing, then, is to let them emerge. Trust yourself and your inner resources.

Rule #2. Find the way to enter into the phantasy that best suits you. You can do these phantasies by yourself. You can read the phantasy to yourself, pausing to give attention to, or to jot down in the spaces provided, the imagery that is taking shape within you. Or you can have someone else take you through the phantasy, asking the questions provided at two or three minute intervals. (If someone is serving you this way, please agree with the person ahead of time that you have every right to stop or not answer when that is the way you feel about it.) Or, if you have access to a cassette recorder, you may want to read the phantasy on tape and play it to yourself, allowing yourself appropriate time to respond.

While engaged in the phantasy remember simply to let it come—unthought and unanalyzed. There will be time to think about it later. Keep alive and attentive to the phantasy and its life during this time.

Rule #3. Ask yourself what the phantasy might mean. Okay, you've had the phantasy. Now what do you do with it? How is it interpreted? Unlike night dreams which are usually not controlled, these phantasies are quite limited. Most times they can be interpreted by plain common sense. The first question to ask is "What might it mean to me?" And the second question is "What else might it mean for me?" You will see examples of this in the phantasies themselves given in later chapters.

Usually the content, the events, and the details of the phantasy are not very important in themselves. The significance of the content, what it might *mean*, is very important.

The primary clue to determining meaning, the magnetic needle pointing north, is a rigorously honest answer to: How was I feeling in the phantasy? Serene? Anxious? Afraid? Jealous? Happy? Irritable? Okay? Sad? What? Pay attention to your feeling tone. (Use adjectives to describe it. Reasons are a dead–end in this context). How were you feeling? Then, in that context, what might the phantasy mean to you?

I'd strongly encourage your telling the phantasy to someone

who knows you and whom you trust, or to some counsellor or mentor. Although telling makes you vulnerable, it also opens you to intimacy, trust, and deeper friendship. Like all valuable things in life, such sharing has its costs. Let the trusted person explore with you what the phantasy might mean until its meaning clicks into place for you. When the meaning surfaces, the content will make some sense to you.

If you can't find any meaning to the phantasy, maybe you are blocking or denying something unpalatable. Maybe you are not able to deal with the meaning at this time. Usually an ordinary, common sense meaning is not too difficult to find. Sometimes further insights come later.

To summarize Rule #3, then: After noting how you feel (that's the compass needle, not the point of arrival) ask yourself: what might it mean? When the meaning of it for your life emerges, and fits you, decide either: I like my life this way . . . I'll keep it; *or* I don't like it . . . I'll work to replace it; *or* I do and don't like it for me . . . I'll change some parts of it.

There's not only deeper self–knowledge in this process; there's deeper, genuine self–love in using one's freedom of choice well.

Whether you intend using the phantasies by yourself, with people you know, or as a group facilitator, it is good to be aware that phantasy is a very creative means of internal communication—internal to the person phantasizing. Phantasies transcend time and space. They are extraordinarily intimate and, at the same time, provide individual, subjective interpretation of reality: your self, your life, your world. Using phantasies is no parlor game.

As you read, or do, the phantasies you will note five steps inherent in them. It is very important not to skip any of the steps, although they can be adapted to serve better the nature of the phantasy, the person, or the group doing them.

First, take a few moments to relax. Being comfortable and relaxed will help you to attend only to the phantasy. Second, pay close attention to the suggestions and questions proper to the phantasy. The guidance they provide (when combined with time for response) enables the phantasy to have its intended effect. At the same time, remember that the phantasy is quite personal. How it works out will be personal to you. Third, give whatever time is needed for the imagery to emerge. People tell me (and it is my own experience) that they "see" things whole. In fact, usually it takes longer to repeat the phantasy aloud than to have it. Still, some time is needed for the perceptions to emerge within the person. Fourth, always allow yourself time to reenter the present time and place. Remember, phantasy transcends time and space. If another dimension of time is experienced by the persons phantasizing, they need time to come back to this time, this place. That's very important gently to insist upon—either with yourself alone, with another person, or with a group. And finally, fifth, take extra time to complete the phantasy, to let what has occurred become more fully conscious. This requires talking, or thinking, or writing about it. Most learning takes place at this point.

You will see, when reading the phantasies that follow, how people get further insights when they verbalize their phantasies. At all times, however, the phantasizer *must* be left free to engage in the phantasy or not—to verbalize it or not. If you are doing the phantasy, it is your right and, in a real sense, is a true love of yourself not to allow yourself to be pushed into revealing those intimate things you don't want to reveal. If you are using these phantasies with a group, unless you are in a mental health profession, be extremely careful not to push or probe others.

One additional word to those of you who might want to use these phantasies with groups. Some years ago professional people in applied behavioral sciences grew quite concerned with the ways phantasies and nonverbal techniques were being used in groups. They articulated several suggestions for responsible use of these techniques in groups.

For one thing, phantasies are not used apart from a particular setting. There's a "before" and an "after." That is to say, they are used in context of a larger design, or in context of the person's own life. Using them to help individuals better understand that context can often be helpful. For example, when someone is struggling to explain a relationship and it's getting wordy and endless, "on the one hand," "on the other hand," and "on the other hand," far beyond the usual number of hands, I'm likely to intervene with a phantasy on relationships. Then I'll continue with the problem under discussion. If used in a group, it is best utilized as a means of contributing to the goal of that session. If working in a group, especially if the people are not well known to you, the meaning and purpose of the phantasy should be explained to them, and they have an equal right to engage in it or not—to talk about it or not.

If you are leading others in phantasy, it is strongly advised that you yourself have some prior experience and instruction in using phantasies.

I find that phantasies are a powerful way to become more aware of dimensions of our lives which might not be clear to us. It is a useful tool. What we decide to do with what we learn from them is what is most important for us.

To make this story short: one ordinary, "everybody has it," human ability is imagination. Even without conscious effort imagination helps connect or link our external senses with our internal perceptions, emotions, thoughts, and values. With its help we can not only recall the past as information, but we can also go over the past as it affects us now, and freely make more mature decisions about how our life will be lived in the future. And there is more. We can use our ability to imagine, to reach those parts of our past and present which escape immediate availability. Simply and quickly we can get a better view of what kind of human beings we are, and what makes us do what we do. With the freedom such knowledge brings, we can then choose, in a more mature way, life as we will.

There is also an unexpected bonus in using phantasy: new self–assurance and freedom. I meet people who, after we know each other a bit, sort of mumble, "I'm not sure I want to go down deep inside of me." Experience tells me that there are two reasons for this: (1) Fear—"If I go down deep inside, I'll find nobody home. Nothing there. I'll find me empty. A nobody. I'd rather not know." (2) Fear—"If I go down deep inside, I'll find out *they* are right. *They* always said I'd amount to nothing. *They* always said I'm no good. *They* always said. . . . I don't want to find out that *they* are right."

Well, I say to my companions in fear, "Suppose you and they are wrong? Will you permit me to walk with you so that together we can find out if there are, indeed, real monsters there, or if all that noise comes from mice with megaphones?"

Since phantasms just about always emerge when we allow them to, they can be drawn upon over and over and over again. How rich, how varied, how endless are our own internal resources. How different our phantasies are from others'. How valid and freeing our phantasies are in their uniqueness. How well they fit us—for, not only are they ours, they are in some ways us. Knowing from experience the wealth of our internal resources is very good reassurance and a fine dissolver of fear.

Part II

THE PHANTASIES

EXPLORING YOURSELF
The Store

As you are about to begin this phantasy, take time to make yourself comfortable. Loosen any tight clothing. Remove your glasses and, if you wish, your shoes. Sit or lie comfortably. Now take a few deep breaths slowly. Let the activities of the day go each time you breathe. When thoughts come to you, acknowledge them and gently return to the silence of your breathing.

Imagine yourself in a store. It is a pleasant store—attractively appointed, comfortable, uncrowded. As you wander up and down the aisles you find all sorts of things you like, not in any special order, but all very appealing to you. Walk around a bit looking at things. ⊶——⊷

As you are walking around you begin to notice a remarkable difference in this store. Not only are there objects, but qualities, values, and principles are also to be found on the shelves. Perhaps they are there in token or symbol, but you have the conviction that you can select what you want and it is really there. Keep looking. ⊶——⊷

Now you decide to select one thing. You pick the one thing you have wanted in your life very much. *What do you select?*

Look at what you have chosen. Examine it carefully. Is it really *the* important thing in your life now? If not, you have time to replace it and select something else which you want even more.

Now take your one important choice to the front of the store. Near the door the owner of the store is waiting for you. You show the owner what you wish to take. The storekeeper looks at your purchase carefully, looks at you carefully, and tells you what it will cost. For the first time you notice that there is no cash register. What the store owner tells you as cost is something very precious to you. *What is demanded as the price of your selection?*

How do you respond to the cost?

Now let the phantasy fade. As you are ready, come back to this time, this place. Stretch if you feel like it. And yawn.
How do you feel?

Using your "right now" feeling as an indicator, *what did you learn about yourself from this phantasy?*

I would encourage you to share this phantasy with a family member or friend who knows you and cares about you. It is very likely that someone can help you understand it even more fully.

One woman told me that when I said she could find "values, principles" in the store as well as things, she was delighted. For a while she had been experiencing herself as a bit short of faith, so she promptly picked up more faith. But when asked if that was what she *really* wanted most, she found herself putting it down and selecting forgiveness instead. The storekeeper, she said, looked *at* her—no, more *through* her—and asked her for her perfectionism.

Another person picked inner peace as the primary thing for her to purchase. She, too, changed her mind and took instead wholeness. What the storekeeper required of her was trust. "Okay," was her response, "but may I pay for it on the installment plan?"

One man wanted freedom. Given another option, he still wanted freedom. What the store owner asked him for was his wife.

"I shopped and shopped and was delighted when I found humor on the shelf," said one friend. "When you said, 'Is that what you really want?' I said, "YES" so vehemently I couldn't believe myself. So I reluctantly dropped it and picked openness." My reluctant colleague brought openness to the storekeeper and was asked to be prepared to suffer loss of good name and reputation.

Self–confidence was the first choice of another lady. Given a chance to keep it or not, she surprised herself by leaving it for wisdom. She was in for another surprise when the storekeeper asked her to surrender her self–confidence as the cost of wisdom.

An old lady loved the big green hat with golden bows. She kept with her first selection. But when the storekeeper asked her for her little gold first communion ring she went into a dither. In her phantasy she never left the store, so undecided was she.

A man wanted power. He had trouble at the door because he couldn't see any face, or hear any voice, of the storekeeper. All he saw was a large white apron, and a hand reaching for his checkbook.

"I want better communication skills," said one teacher. She kept to her first choice. What was required of her was her anger.

And one person who chose to be a clown was asked for her security. Agreement was reached in spite of some serious apprehension.

This phantasy is good for surfacing current values. I find it especially valuable in terms of realism.

For one thing, it shows what the person truly is concerned about rather than something intruding itself. For instance, one girl first chose graduate study for her purchase. When she looked it over she replaced it and picked a hug. She said that she realized that she really wanted to work with people for a while before continuing her formal education.

The phantasy is realistic in terms of the price required for the goods selected. And the person having the phantasy generally is more realistic in phantasy about implementing what is required than when speaking from a more decision–making stance. Many people find the price "difficult" or "scary." While they are generally willing to pay it, they find themselves saying to the storekeeper, "bit by bit," "with reservation," "I can't do it all at once, but I will make good."

Most are satisfied with their resolution of the phantasy. The few who suffer from indecision (like the lady with the green hat and the first communion ring) become more aware of the challenge to identify what is really important to them in their current situation.

EXPLORING YOURSELF
The Cave

Find a quiet and dimly lighted place. Make yourself comfortable by loosening any tight clothing or belt, removing your shoes and eyeglasses. Now sit or lie comfortably. Feel yourself sinking into the surface which supports your body. After taking a few deep breaths, breathe slowly and easily. Attend only to your breathing. If other thoughts come let them, acknowledge them, and pay them no further notice. Just breathe.

Imagine yourself with several friends on a camping trip. While that may or may not be your style, but remember that everything is possible in imagination. You come to a small valley and although it is early, you decide to stay there for the rest of the day. Find the valley and the meadow where you will camp.

It's early afternoon. You look at the nearest mountain and want to climb it. There's time. You ask, but none of your friends want to go. So you decide to go alone and that's okay with you. Gather what you will need. Start the walk up the mountain.

The path is well marked. You have no difficulty following it. In fact, you are rather glad your friends decided to stay behind. Enjoy the walk through the woods.

As you go higher the woods begin to thin and the terrain becomes rockier. You are confident that you can handle it and continue to enjoy the challenge. Only now you become aware that you have forgotten something important. *What did you forget? What will that mean for you?*

41

Now the pathway is very narrow indeed. It is wide enough for you as long as you stay very close to the mountainside. To the right is a long drop down. Around a curve on the path stands a sturdy mountain goat. You need to get past him, and you will. *How do you get past the mountain goat?*

The rest of the way up is uneventful. Someone had told you, you remembered, there's an interesting cave at the top of the mountain. You decide it's worth a try looking for. Look for the cave. ⊶——⊷

You do find it. Unexpectedly you find something else. Two ferocious looking monsters are guarding the cave entrance. At this point you really want to go into the cave. *How do you get past the two monsters?*

You are inside the cave. Walk around and explore it. What's it like? To your surprise you find something there with your name on it. What do you find? During the exploration you find an opening into another cave. You go into the inner cave. You're in for another surprise. Someone is there, waiting for you. *Who's there?*

What goes on between the two of you?

Now retrace your steps. Go through the outer cave . . . , past the monsters . . . , down the mountain . . . , back to camp and your friends.

Let the phantasy fade.

Come back to this room and this time. As you are ready, sit up. You may want to yawn and stretch. Then begin to think about the phantasy, or tell it to someone.

Campers love the beginning of the phantasy. Others are amused at the thought of themselves in this situation. Some like it, some don't. *How did you respond to being in this situation?*

What did you forget? How important was that for you? Some say they forgot a canteen for water. And immediately got thirsty. Perhaps they stayed thirsty, blaming themselves for being stupid or blaming their friends for not having reminded them. Perhaps they found a stream and took care of their thirst that way. People often say they forgot a flashlight and just plain hope they won't need one. Others name ropes, and cleats (so they will have to find easier ways to climb); knives (and hope they won't need one—although one man went back to get one); a sweater (one woman walked faster when she realized this).

The important thing here is not what you forgot but how you reacted to the oversight. Did you accept responsibility for it? Or, did you blame your friends for not having taken care of you? Or, did you make a big fuss with yourself, not accepting your own limitation and mistake?

The other important factor here is what you did about the forgotten object. Could you reasonably go on without it? If so, did you go back anyway because you are very cautious? If not, did you go on anyway, being somewhat rash? Did you find another way to deal with the situation (like the man who found a stream to slake his thirst)? Attend to how you dealt with the difficulty of your own forgetfulness.

Then there was the mountain goat. His territory. How did you get past him? One athletic young man grabbed the goat by the horns, gave a mighty twist and hurled him into space. That's about what he does with anything that has the misfortune of getting in his way. A sturdy girl kept her eye on the goat and used her equipment to scale the wall above him and climb over him. One woman told him she had to keep going. When the goat didn't move she scolded him, and pushed him backwards along the path until it was wide enough for her to pass. "What was the goat doing?" I asked her. "Glaring at me, but moving," was her answer. She caught her breath and giggled a bit. "Why, he looked like my pastor . . . and that is how I treat him. . . . Oh!" Another person fed the goat; still another scared him away. One told the goat that there was this great cave on the top of the mountain. Why didn't they form a partnership and split whatever they found? Some treat the goat politely. "Please, Mr. Goat, would you let me pass?" Others try persuasion. A youngster got on the goat's back and rode him. What did you do? What might that tell you about the way you handle things?

Well, you got to the top of the mountain. How were you feeling while searching for the cave? Adventurous? Enjoying it? Dismal—just another task? Hoping you would find it? Hoping you wouldn't? How? Is that the way you usually feel when searching for—whatever? And what might that tell you about yourself?

Monsters! Of all things in this day and age, monsters! What were the monsters like that were guarding the cave? Describe them. In retrospect, do they remind you of anyone? Often they don't; sometimes they do. If so, what are your monsters protecting so you can't get there?

How did you get by the monsters? The brash young man, who flipped the mountain goat off the cliff, killed the monsters. Most people don't. Most either distract them by enticing them away, creating a disturbance for them to investigate, or by giving them food. A few try persuasion. One woman just walked up ("I felt very confident, because I knew I was meant to go into that cave"), looked the two of them in the eye and said, "I'm safe. I won't hurt anything in the cave. And I am meant to go into the cave. Please let me pass." They did. Another woman just sat there and cried. The monsters came over and comforted her. (So do other people.) The one who had made a deal with the goat to split the contents of the cave, let the goat handle the monsters. What did you do? How does that reflect the way you generally approach barriers, especially when the barrier is someone in authority?

What was the inside of your cave like? For one man, "It's 'just a cave.' You know, rocks and dirt and animal droppings." That's all he found, except for his name, like graffiti, on the wall. (It's "just life," too, for the way he tends to live.) In contrast, another found stalactites and stalagmites, "and all those neat things." A girl found something to give contest to Ali Baba's cave. Bright, full of lights and treasures. She had an exciting time looking around. A glittering stone unicorn is what she found. "I *love* unicorns!" and she smiled the rest of the time. The woman who had told the monster she was safe and wanted to go in found a white leather covered Bible with her name on it in gold. Her response was somewhat rueful, "I really should spend more time with God's Word." A box of tools was there for one man. "That does it! I will go for those carpentry lessons!" What did you find? What might it mean to you? And—important—what does it show you about your expectations? Rocks, dirt, and animal droppings? Or something good, interesting, contributing to your well–being? What *are* your expectations in an uncertain situation?

Who did you find in the inner cave? Someone friendly or hostile? Someone you were glad to see? Afraid of? Wanted to avoid? Surprised? A young girl began to cry when she entered the inner cave. Her runaway brother was there. She said later she hadn't let herself miss him much, because her parents were so angry at him. The phantasy let her feel how much she loved him, and she decided to contact him. A man found his boss, of whom he was afraid. After their conversation some things cleared up for him. Another found a boyhood enemy lying in wait for him. They had a fight, and to his surprise, he won. For him, the insight was that things weren't the same now as when he was a child. He had grown up.

Some find a person whom they loved, who has died, and they settle some unfinished business. (Often enough it is as simple as telling the other one, "I love you.") People find friends there. Sometimes they converse, sometimes they go on exploring together, sometimes they return to camp with them. A few stay unsettled in the relationship.

Who was in the inner cave for you? Note whether the person was friendly or hostile to you. What might that indicate about the way you meet people? Pay attention to how you related with that person. Chances are it was quite spontaneous and therefore quite revealing of your style. What went on? What might that show you?

This phantasy is very good for surfacing how you deal with obstacles, how you react when the other one is stronger, surer, or in authority. It also identifies habitual expectations— anticipation of "how it will be." Interesting, boring? Expected, unexpected? Friendly, harmful? Have you any further insights into your own attitudes?

EXPLORING YOURSELF
The Wise Person

Stand and take a good, hard stretch. Then, with your hands locked behind your neck, bend slowly to the left, up, and slowly to the right, several times. Then stretch again, all the time taking deep, slow breaths.

Make yourself comfortable. Remove your glasses and shoes. Loosen any tight clothing. Feel yourself sink into the chair or bed or floor. Attend to your breathing, letting other thoughts come as they will, acknowledging them, and letting them go. Breathe slowly and smoothly.

Picture yourself out in the country on a lovely summer day. You are alone and feeling quite well. A well–defined path is just to your right. It disappears among the trees. You decide to take a walk following the path.

It's pleasant in the woods. There are the usual sounds of birds and insects. A rabbit runs across your path. Sunlight makes pretty shadows among the leaves. You continue to walk along the winding pathway.

A clearing comes into sight. It's rather sunny. On a log to one side, under a tree, someone is sitting. Somehow you know that this is indeed a wise person. With some delight, you approach the person and stand there a moment. The person beckons you to be seated on the log. You do so.

After some silence, you turn to the wise person and ask something that's been on your mind. *What do you ask?*

There is silence again. Then the wise person turns to you and answers. *What is the answer?*

Remembering that anything is possible in imagination, you begin gently to experience a change. While you remain seated on the log, you also become the wise person. As the wise person, look at yourself. *How do you feel about you? Do you say anything to you? If so, what?*

Now you are entirely you on the log and the wise person is back. You look at each other intently. *What happens?*

Now bid the wise person good–bye. Cross the clearing, find the path, reenter the woods. Follow the path back to where you began your walk. When you are there, come back to this room. Sit or stand slowly, stretch, and yawn if you want.

Begin to think or talk about the phantasy.

What was it like for you to start walking along the path through the woods?

Many people enjoy it. Sometimes people are afraid. One city woman told me she saw eyes peeking out from behind every tree. Another delighted in the birds. Several picked flowers. Many just looked and smelled. A few felt a sense of urgency to "get somewhere." How was the walk for you?

When you saw the wise person, was it someone you recognized or not? Sometimes the wise person becomes someone else. Did that happen? Often the wise person is a parent/spouse, a clergyperson, one who has served the phantasizer in some capacity as a mentor. Some people see Jesus. Occasionally the Blessed Mother is the wise person. At times it is a totally unknown person, generally aged and serene. Who was your wise person? Were you surprised?

When you first sat on the log beside the wise person, how did you feel? One man said, "As if I had come home." A boy reported, "Antsy. I was sort of embarrassed to be near to him!" First a girl said, "I kept trying to think of something to say, but I was full up and no words would come." Others used words like "good," "okay," "strange," "oh, I like it," "very comfortable."

One woman noticed, "The woods weren't quiet at all. Neither was my heart. But when my wise person looked at me, I felt very serene. . . ."

What did you ask the wise person?

Sometimes people say they surprised themselves with what they asked. One woman said she started to ask if she should go back to graduate school, and instead heard herself saying, "How do you really know what is important in life?" A young man was going to ask about how to build his body when he asked "What does it mean . . . life, what does it mean anyway?" People ask about their families, their jobs, and their future. Many are serious questions about the meaning and purpose of life, the existence of God, values.

What was the wise person's response to you?

Generally, if the phantasizer is freely into the phantasy, the response is quite personal. Often it is so obvious it is surprising. Sometimes it is so unexpected, or unexpectedly simple, the phantasizer is startled into a smile. Occasionally the wise person just looks at the phantasizer and the look is answer enough.

What was your answer? How did you react to the answer?

When you changed into the wise person looking at yourself, how did you feel? Recalling that feeling tone is important.

One young person said, "Disgusted. I was playing it cool and being so phony I couldn't look at me much." A woman said, "Sad. I had wasted a good deal of energy on unimportant things. I see that now." Another woman said, "I wanted to hug and comfort me." A man remarked, "It was sort of surprising to see me. I felt uneasy, wondering what I was doing there."

How did you feel, as a wise person, looking at you?

When you and the wise person were separate again, what happened when you looked at each other?

People's responses are as varied as their questions. Some embraced. Some wept. Others made a remark about their first question and articulated an insight that had come. "I see now that I have to do something for myself." "I guess I should have asked you how to go about taking off the mask." Some felt very happy and tranquil. One invited the wise person home to meet her family. Another couldn't scoot away fast enough.

What happened when you and the wise person looked at each other? Bade farewell?

This phantasy is useful for identifying, not what might be most immediately pressing in your life, but what is significantly important to you. Often people articulate the real issue the first time. At times the deeper concern surfaces when the wise person looks at you—or when you, having become the wise person—look at yourself. It's a good phantasy for dropping masks in areas of real concern.

Occasionally people come to a more conscious realization of how they regard someone as a wise person. It may be startling. Usually it's quite satisfying.

Thinking back over the whole phantasy, what impressions do you have now?

EXPLORING YOURSELF
The Hospital

This phantasy will take a little longer than some of the others. It will reveal more, too. I'd suggest you use it when you want to get some clarity on what is uppermost in your mind and heart, and who is more important to you in those matters. I'll say more about that at the end of the phantasy.

Make yourself physically comfortable. Take time to stretch and yawn. Loosen any clothing that may be tight. Remove your shoes and glasses if you have them, and either lie down or sit easily.

Breathe slowly and deeply several times. Then breathe at a comfortable pace attending only to your breathing. As other thoughts and concerns come to your mind, acknowledge them and let them go. Return your attention to your breathing.

Imagine yourself at home in your bedroom. You are winding down after a long day. Perhaps you have a cup of coffee, or a drink in your hand. Maybe you are reading a bit, or listening to some music before going to sleep. At any rate, you are preparing for a good night's sleep and you are quite relaxed.

You settle comfortably in bed. The lights are out. All is quiet. Just as you are dozing off, the phone rings.

You get up to answer the phone. The woman's voice is unknown to you. She introduces herself as a nurse at a local hospital. What she says to you is this: "We have an emergency patient here—actually, a very famous person. The patient is critical. All that we hear is your name. This famous person keeps calling for you. Are you willing to come to the hospital right away? It is urgent."

Do you go to the hospital?

If not, if you go back to bed, let the phantasy end here.

If you do go to the hospital, get yourself there. You are met at the door and brought into the person's room. You approach the bed. Lying there, critical, you see—yourself.

Carry on a conversation with yourself in the bed. ⊶⟶⊶

Suddenly doctors and nurses are scurrying in with equipment. They tell you they have work to do. They tell you to leave the room. *What do you do?*

Whatever has happened, you do return to yourself in the bed, and your standing–up–self and your self–in–bed merge and become one. You go to the side of the room where you see a huge heart on the wall. You go into the heart. *What is it like for you?*

Stay relaxed, and let this part of the phantasy fade. Still in imagination, tell what has happened during the phantasy to someone. ⊶⟶⊶

Now, as you are ready, let the phantasy fade. Come back to this room and this time. You might want to stretch. When you are ready, go over the phantasy. You can do it alone or with a family member or friend who cares for you.

Actually this phantasy has five parts or purposes:

(1) Did you go to the hospital (at some real inconvenience to yourself)? If so, or if not, why?

(2) Whatever came up in the initial conversation between the visiting–you and the you–in–bed is important to you in your life now. What was your conversation about?

(3) When the medical team came in and wanted to work, what was your response? It is significant in terms of how you control your life. Do you let other people take over? The phantasy is imagination, so you might have coped in any number of ways. Whatever you did, what might it tell you

about your ownership of your life?

(4) Going into the heart surfaces raw present emotions. What was your feeling as whatever happened, happened?

(5) To whom did you tell the phantasy? At this point in your life, that person is important to you in some way.

Let's go through the questions one at a time, and the ways in which some people have responded to them.

(1) Do you go to the hospital or not? What was your response to an inconvenient call to go to an unnamed person? What you did at this time is somewhat less important than *why* you did it. In my experience virtually all of the people went to the hospital. Many are just plain generous. Generosity can be laced with curiosity, or perhaps, some satisfaction that a *famous* person is calling for you. Several people have said that they found it less bothersome to respond to the call than to live with the guilt of saying "no." However you responded, do pay some attention to your motivation.

(2) How did you feel seeing yourself in bed? Some people sort of expected it; most are surprised; occasionally people name the person they expected to see there and indeed do see that person before being told it is "you." If you find another person there, take a hard look at the influence, the power, that person has over your life. Do you want that to remain true?

When the visiting–you speaks with the critically–ill/ injured–you, what sorts of things do you talk about? I've heard people say, "All that fuss over expectations and what people want from you isn't really that important."

"Tell Ann how much I love her."

"Go away, I don't want anything. I just want to die."

"I'm sorry for the way I treated you." . . . "That's mutual."

"You know you are going to die, don't you? Do you want to pray?"

"What does it all mean, anyway? I never make any difference."

"I'm tired. I don't care."

"I've really wasted a lot of time on things that aren't that important."

"Why does it have to be this way?"

"I really like you. We've been through a lot of things together—and now this. I'm glad you're here."

"Will you hear my confession and anoint me?" (Clergy tend to say this. They call it an occupational hazard.)

Whatever you spoke about, it had to be something important to you, or some attitude that is affecting your life now. Attend to it.

(3) When the medical team came in, what did you do? Some people leave immediately. Some fade into the woodwork but stay with their critical selves. Others ask to stay. Some fight and order the medical people to get out, or to work around them saying the visiting–I is more important to the bedridden–I than outsiders. Some do it peaceably, some violently.

The crucial question here is What did you do? It is significant for your habitual ownership of your life. Do *you* decide who decides for you? And secondly, how do you go about it? Meekly? Angrily? With negotiation? Sullenly? Decisively?

(4) What was the heart like for you? A big valentine? Concrete? Pulsating and anatomically real? . . .

What did you do?

"It was like a concrete alcove and I could barely go in."

"It was a huge heart, and I got into it by walking through an artery first. It was pumping blood on the heartbeat and somehow I wasn't afraid. Even when the chamber filled up and I was surrounded by blood, it was full of love and peace. I didn't even have trouble breathing but felt very loving and loved."

"My in–bed–self and visiting–self didn't merge. We went into the heart together and it was so gross—all that blood— that we had to leave and wash up. Then we went back and just laughed and laughed. I guess I really didn't get into it."

"My father was in there, and machinery. I realized my

father had a heart, and did the best he could. Even if that best was treating me mechanically. But I knew he did have a heart."

"The heart was like a big, golden glow. With its beating I kept hearing the words, 'Take heart, take heart.' And I knew I wouldn't give up, that *I* would be unfinished if I did."

"The heart I went into had a long hallway. The first room was very clean and sterile, like the hospital. I didn't like it. The second room was baroque—very overfurnished, plushy, heavy, oppressive. I didn't like that one either. The third room opened to the out–of–doors—woods and a stream. I started to go out where I could breathe."

"The heart was the Sacred Heart of Jesus. I met him in there. Really, I was surprised that it all was so easy."

"When I got into the heart, it was like having a transfusion. My weaknesses were being drained out. I was being filled with energy. Love. Life. I liked being there."

Sometimes going into the heart brings insight. Almost always it surfaces the dominant emotion in your present circumstances. What was it like for you?

(5) To whom did you tell the phantasy? Spouse? Friend? For one man—recently hospitalized—it was his oldest sister. They had become friends during his post–operative "period."

Sometimes people can't find anyone to tell. If that happened to you, go back over the initial conversation you had when you first found yourself in bed. And go over the way you felt going into the heart. What might that suggest? If you can, do find someone you can trust to talk it through.

All in all, in this phantasy there is opportunity to see how you see yourself and issues important to you. How you responded to your in–bed you, and what you talked about is at the heart of this phantasy's purpose. What is of great significance to you? What in your life do you most regret having done? Or, not done? Is what you talked about superficial and trivial? Are you satisfied with yourself?

Another purpose of the phantasy is to articulate how you take control of your life. If you left the room when the medical team came in, you might be defending yourself now.

You can make a good case for it, too. But think a moment. That you YOU in bed, and YOU were allowing yourself to be dismissed. How do you take charge of your own life?

Thirdly, the heart on the wall is designed to surface your present predominant emotional attitude. What did you learn?

Are you satisfied with the depth of your concern about the way your life is being spent? About the responsibility you exercise over it? What might your emotional response indicate? Are there changes you'd want to make? If so, how will you go about making them?

Child under Tree

Before beginning the phantasy, stretch and take a few deep breaths. Take your time, breathe deeply. Find a quiet place which is not brightly lighted and make yourself comfortable. Attend to your breathing, slowly, regularly. As other thoughts come, acknowledge them and let them go. Just pay attention to your breathing.

Imagine yourself out in the country on a bright day in June. The sky is a beautiful, deep blue. Puffy clouds are scudding across it. There is a cool breeze. You are very comfortable. Although you are alone in the country, you are enjoying your own company.

There is a dirt road near you, one with grass and weeds on both sides and in the middle. Start walking along the road. You are aware of the noises of insects, small animals, and birds. Continue your walk.

There's a bend in the road. When you go around it, you see, a bit ahead of you, a child sitting under a tree. Walk toward the child.

As you get closer you become aware that that child is you. The child under the tree is you at age five or six. Go to the child and greet your six–year–old self.

Your child self looks up at you and asks: "How did I get to be you?" *Answer your six–year–old self.*

Then your child self says, "Will it always be like this?" *What do you say?*

Then your child self probes you still further. "What might be different?" What might be different? *What do you suggest to your six–year–old self?*

Now the time is coming to leave. Say good–bye to your little child self. ⊶——⊷

Leave the child. . . . Start walking down the road you first took . . . around the bend . . . back to where you started.

Let the phantasy fade. Come back to this time, this place. As you are ready, stretch. You might want to yawn and stretch again. Now begin to think or talk about your phantasy.

Some people don't remember themselves that young. If it should happen that you are one who doesn't remember back to age five or six, you might want to try the phantasy at whatever age you *can* go back to. Some people aren't clear about if they *really* remember, or if they remember being told about things, or if they merely associate with pictures in the family album. That isn't particularly important for the purpose of the phantasy. What is important is that, in speaking to ourselves as children, the conversation is honest. For most of us, there is little threat in talking to ourselves and especially to ourselves at a young age.

How did you greet yourself? Occasionally people "know," even before it is said, that it is themselves they are to find beneath the tree. Some already have a son or daughter or grandchild pictured there, and have to shift gears. That is all right. Others are surprised to find themselves there. Some are pleased; others are saddened. What is important is that you are aware of how it was for you when you met yourself as a child. How did you respond to each other? What was the impact on you?

When your five– or six–year–old self looked at you and asked, "How did I get to be you?" how did you feel? Were you glad to think about it, or embarrassed? Excited? Ho hum? Sad? How were you?

Many people are glad that someone is interested enough to

ask them and relieved to put it into words. Some get teary, and give way to a sense of waste or loneliness or failure. Others will say something like, "It wasn't easy, kid, but let me tell you. . . ." One woman said her child self anticipated her. When she went to greet the little girl, the child said, "Let's go exploring." She remembered that, as a child, she and her brothers and sister loved to "explore" in the woods. So when her child self asked, "How did I get to be you?" she laughingly answered, "By exploring." And realized with delight how true it was.

A man said, "By hard work. . . . But, you know, it wasn't all work. In fact. . . ." Another man responded, "I don't know. It just sorta happened. You know, you finish school, you have to get a job. . . . It just sorta happened." Still another male phantasizer blurted out, "By fighting. I fought for everything I have today!"

Many people say they see their lives almost like a large fresco, all at once. Sometimes one part emerges more strongly than another; sometimes it seems to be all of a piece. What is quite consistent in this part of this phantasy is the candor of the answers. How did you answer your child self?

"Will it always be like this?"

"I hope so!" exclaimed the woman who spends her life exploring. "I expect I'll be exploring for other things, but I hope I'll never lose the anticipation of finding something interesting, the excitement of looking, the surprise at what I find—even though sometimes I don't like it."

Will it always be like this? Much of the answer to this depends on how satisfied (not complacent, but satisfied) you are with yourself now. The exploring woman wasn't complacent—stuck and agreeable to be in a rut. She keeps going on to and enjoying new things. The hardworking man expects to go on working hard, but had a new awareness of other pleasures and satisfactions in his life. What might be different for him is giving himself permission to enjoy more his own legitimate pleasures.

When the other man claimed, "I don't know. It just sorta happened," there is evidence of an abdication of responsibility for the controls of his own life. The man who said that was somewhat startled at his own words. He began to wonder, indeed, if it will always be like this. Wonder was also the reaction of the one who "fought for everything I have today." In a musing way he muttered, "My wife tells me I don't have to fight so much. That things can come more easily. I don't know. . . ."

What might be different for you? What insight might that give you into your own self–satisfaction or lack of it? Into your own attitudes toward life right now?

"What might be different?"

More attitudes emerge with this question. So do some very deep desires. "I want to slow down and enjoy things more," was one man's response. The "I wonder ifs . . ." which grow out of the previous question sometimes take the form of "I want. . . ."; "I'll try. . . ."; "I'm going to. . . ."; "I'm going to try to see the other guy's point of view and maybe get along better without fighting so much. . . ."; "I'm going to make some of my own decisions more clearly, and stick to them." One woman had said she got to be the way she is "by the grace of God." When she had to answer "What might be different," she caught her breath sharply. "I've been ignoring some things in my life and not understanding why other people are irritated with me. I do believe in the grace of God. I think I had better pay better attention to what I do and don't do with it. And maybe pay more attention to what in me irritates others."

What might be different for you? What do you intend to *do* about it?

When it was time to say good–bye to your five– or six–year–old self, how did you go about it?

For some people it was time to go. The visit was a good one and termination was natural. Others want to give advice and, almost simultaneously, realize the futility of it. They tend to think some more about what might be different. Still others assure the child that things will turn out okay. Some of them begin to internalize that belief and start to make some positive change. A few people find it very hard to say good–bye. They don't want to leave the child self.

In my experience this is a particularly good phantasy to

talk over with another person. In the talking about it, it's quite possible that some new things will emerge.

One woman, who began by saying what a happy phantasy it was for her, surprised herself by bursting into tears in telling it. Suddenly a sense of loss overwhelmed her. The location of her phantasy was a real place where her family had picnicked on Sundays for several years. What struck her was the fact that her parents were dead and how the rest of the family had scattered. Her "what might be different" took a new turn. She was going to call the rest of her family more often.

A man who had become very teary saying good–bye to his little boy self took a deep breath and declared, "It's about time I grew up." Another one smiled softly as he said, "I can go and visit him anytime I want. But I'm living my life now, and by and large, I like it."

Watch your own reaction to your phantasy. Follow whatever new directions suggest themselves. And then evaluate and judge what you will do about them.

EXPLORING YOUR RELATIONSHIPS

The God Tree

The God Tree phantasy is a quick, easy way to perceive how we are relating to God at a particular time in our life. It also shows us how we feel about ourselves. And how important other people are to us in the current situation.

Before beginning a phantasy, it is important to relax. Assume a comfortable physical position. If the environment permits, loosen tight clothing and remove your shoes. Taking a few deep breaths will help the relaxing process. If thoughts come (and generally the day's cares do), acknowledge them and gently let them go. Breathe at a slow, comfortable pace. Direct your attention to breathing for only a few moments. Then begin.

Imagine yourself in summer, somewhere out–of–doors. It might be a place familiar to you, or it might not. But the weather is pleasant . . . you are alone . . . you like being there and alone. Find yourself in a pleasant, outdoor place in summer. ⊶⟶⊷

As you are enjoying being alone out–of–doors, you begin to realize something. (Anything is possible in imagination, you know.) So, gently, you become aware that God is appearing to you as a tree. A tree is God. Let that tree slowly come into focus for you. ⊶⟶⊷

What kind of tree is your God tree?

How does it look?

Perhaps something is going on around it. If there is, *what is happening around your God tree?*

As you are noticing your God tree, you slowly and gently become aware that you are a tree. What kind of tree are you? Let it come to you, let it come into focus. ⊶——⊷

What is your tree like?

Where is it in relation to the God tree?

Perhaps something is going on in or near your tree. If so, *what is happening around your tree?*

Are there any other trees near you or the God tree? Are there any other trees in sight? (Maybe yes, maybe no.) If so, *what are they like?*

Is anything happening near them?

Now come out of the phantasy slowly. Let the phantasy fade. Come back to this room, this time. If you want to yawn or stretch, do so. People often like to do this after a phantasy.

Then wait a few moments. If possible, verbalize the phantasy. Hearing it spoken will have another impact on you—valuable in its own way—so it is good to tell it to someone you trust.

It is useful to pay attention to several things:

(1) What kind of tree was the God tree? What might that *mean* to you? What kind of associations have you with that kind of tree? What was the condition of the tree: healthy? barren? fruitful? dead? Was it alone? far? near? Was it hospitable to birds? animals? people? aloof? What might these answers *mean* to you?

(2) What kind of tree were you? What might that *mean* to you? What kind of association have you with that kind of tree? What was the condition of the "my" tree—healthy? barren? fruitful? dead? Was it alone? near the God tree? near anything? Was it hospitable to birds? animals? people? aloof? deserted? How did you feel about seeing the "my" tree so situated?

(3) Were there other trees near? in sight? How were they: healthy? barren? fruitful? dead? helpful? threatening? Were they friendly? aloof? What? What feeling did you associate with them?

As I mentioned before, phantasies will assume a variety of shapes and forms. There is no one "right" phantasy. In even a small group of people, there will be widely diverse images.

One woman I know saw God as an apple tree—full of big, ripe apples. There were nests in the tree; squirrels and small animals were round about it. She was a peach tree, also laden with lucious, ripe fruit. Many other trees were in view—all of them fruit or nut trees, all of them heavily productive. Children were playing in the area, and the woman felt just fine. Her phantasy suggests that she is a nurturing woman, one who sees her God as provident, caring, and loving. She sees both herself and others as fruitful. Her phantasy confirms that she is a woman of high self–esteem, friendly, and on good terms with others.

Another woman saw herself as a large spruce next to a house. Her God tree was on the distant horizon—a dead elm.

No other trees were in sight. She said quite outright that she did not know if she believed in God any more, that she certainly had not prayed in years. And no, she neither has nor needs any friends.

In contrast there was a tall, grave man whose God tree was a large, beautiful evergreen. His was a small, "scroungy" holly tree, with few leaves and no berries. All around were many holly trees, all with many leaves and berries. Obviously he thought much of God and others, and not much at all of himself.

One girl couldn't "get God to be a tree. He was a big rock and I was next to him." Her tree was a healthy pine. Behind her was a forest—all burned down. When I asked her who was burned down and no longer alive to her, she burst into tears and said, "My father." Out came her fears and heartaches with respect to her father.

Sometimes people's own trees are bigger than their God tree. One man said, "My God tree was a nice bush but I could not make it grow." That man began to look at trust in providence in his practical, day–to–day living.

One elderly woman in the group was facing a very painful surgical procedure for the ninth time. There was no use telling her it would "be all right." She had had too much painful experience. Besides that, she had other physical complications making the surgery more risky. In her phantasy God was a huge weeping willow. She was a small weeping willow, totally inside the branches of her God tree. No one, nothing else was in sight. The scene was very quiet. She had a sense of being enveloped by love and peace.

A little boy saw the God tree as a big pine full of ripe apples. There was a rainbow above it. Puppies, chipmunks, squirrels were around it. He didn't get to be a tree—he was too busy playing with the small animals under the God tree.

The God tree phantasy can be adapted in other ways. If your major intent is exploring your relationship to God, you might walk around the God tree in the beginning of the phantasy and touch it. (Whether you can or not; or how you touch the tree is immediately significant.) Then you "do something" or "go somewhere." (Sometimes people sit down or sleep under the God tree; sometimes they hide; sometimes they meet friends or loved ones there.)

Another way to extend the phantasy, after noticing if there are any other trees around, is to say: Something happens now. Something is different. *What happens?*

What difference does that make to the God tree?

What happens to you with the change? How has it affected you?

Let the phantasy fade. ⊶⟶⊷

Often the change that people experience in the phantasy is a change of weather (rain or wind storm, snow, lightning); or a change of season; or the change from day to night. These are common responses. Whatever the change, ask again, "What might that mean to me?"

One man saw God as a huge redwood, himself as a small redwood. The God tree was healthy, strong, and "soaking up all the sunlight and water." What happened was that he saw townspeople filing out with axes to get firewood. This man *knew* that he, not the God tree, was going to be axed. "That's not fair of God, taking everything like that!" Then he burst out with, "This is the first time in my life I ever said anything bad about God. And I like it!" Then he paused, and added, "I think I will talk about this with a good friend of mine." I encouraged him to do just that.

One young woman saw a severe storm. Her tree was struck by lightning. Then the God tree grew toward her and prevented her from falling over.

Another woman saw a drought. The roots of her tree reached to the roots of the God tree and were sucking the life out of it. She was a very angry lady whose phantasy helped her to become more aware of how furious she really was with God.

A little girl saw the God tree, her tree, and other trees as all sizes of pines. What changed was that many children came to play around and under them.

When the "something happens" is a change in seasons, or a storm, often enough the "my" tree changes, is hurt, or is protected. The God tree doesn't usually change but is there for the person. Sometimes a person finds an unconsciously strong faith emerging into consciousness. Occasionally, "what changes" is that the "my" tree grows after a difficult situation.

If you are a young man, you might want to use cars or machines instead of trees for the imagery. Toys sometimes are a useful way to phantasize with children. The possibilities are endless.

Images never lie. After a phantasy people often are very relaxed and at peace. In my experience phantasies tend to stay with people a long time. Insights come weeks, even months, later.

For instance, one of the most precious letters I received this past Christmas was from the tall, grave man whose own tree was a "scroungy" holly tree. He wrote, "My holly tree now is in full bloom, and the bees are buzzing all around it."

Relationships

At various times in our lives we have probably spoken the phrase "other people" with tenderness and, at times, with contempt. Although we sometimes look for a way out, there is no escaping the fact that we human beings live out our lives in relationship. It is precisely because of this fact that we do well to occasionally examine our relationships.

Sometimes I am not sure how I am relating with another person. At other times I find myself engaged with someone who expresses hesitancy about another person.

"I don't know what it is about her, but. . . ."

"I don't know if I can trust him."

"I'm afraid if I try it, I'll look like a fool and nothing will come of it anyway—so why bother?"

"I just don't know."

"Oh, he's a good man, but. . . ."

Sometimes how we feel about another is not that simple to explain. We can go back and forth, round and round, explaining how we feel about another person, while never really getting a satisfactory grasp on what we mean. When that is happening I use this phantasy. When you are plagued by uncertainty in a relationship, you might choose to use this phantasy yourself.

Make yourself comfortable. Close your eyes and take a few slow breaths. Attend to your breathing for a few minutes.

⸱⸱⸱⸱⸱⸱⸱⸱⸱⸱⸱⸱⸱⸱⸱⸱⸱⸱⸱⸱⸱⸱⸱⸱⸱⸱⸱⸱⸱⸱⸱⸱⸱⸱⸱⸱

Picture yourself in a room together with the other person. The other person is holding something.
What is the other person holding?

You are holding something.

What are you holding? Look at what the other person is holding, and at what you are holding.

Something happens between the two objects. *What is the interaction between the objects?*

Slowly let the phantasy fade. When you are ready, open your eyes and consider the phantasy. ⊶——⊷

How do you feel? (Note the feeling tone, immediately after the phantasy. It is an important indicator of the relationship.) Then ask yourself:

What was the other person holding?

What were you holding?

What was the interaction?

How were you feeling?

What might that mean?

The meaning is usually quite apparent. For instance, one woman saw the other person holding a book, open to some special place. The one phantasizing hadn't "read" it—but she *knew* it was a special place. She saw herself as holding a rose. Very gently she took the initiative and placed the rose on the book, marking that special passage. After the phantasy she smiled softly and said, "I really didn't know we shared something important with that kind of love."

A boy saw his father and himself in the kitchen. The father was holding a fork and eating. The boy had a broom in his hands. The broom swept the father's plate off the table. The plate broke as it hit the floor, and the food caused the father to slip and fall as he got up from the table. ("And I laughed," said the boy.)

One man said the other person was holding a very beautiful, antique porcelain–covered dish. The man was holding flowers. The flowers pulled him toward the dish, but it was covered. Slowly the cover came off and the dish received the flowers. He looked a little surprised, a little relieved, and then he smiled.

Another woman said the other person was holding flowers and she was holding a large photograph of someone she loved very dearly. The photograph went to the table top and the other person put her flowers in front of the picture. "I guess I do trust her."

"You were holding a book," a lady said to me, "and I had an apple." What happened? "I laughed at a joke in your book and you ate a piece of my apple." We do share a good deal.

One woman was very hesitant about approaching her boss concerning some difficulty in her job. In her perception it was serious, and certainly it was bothering her very much. Yet she was afraid the confrontation might do her more harm than good. "What is he holding?" "A map." "What are you holding?" "A pencil." "What is the interaction?" "The pencil goes through the map." She had an unpleasant, but successful, meeting with her boss.

This phantasy is simple and easy, but I find it helpful in cutting through rationalizing, evasiveness, or vindictiveness. I even use it spontaneously during a conversation to keep me more in touch with what is happening between the other person and me.

One day I had a sense of something not going quite right during a conversation. My friend was intrigued with the idea of phantasy and agreed to do one with me. He saw me holding a glass egg, while he grasped a wooden spatula. Then the glass egg broke the wooden spatula. Dismayed I asked, "What happened today, what did I say that threatened you?" He identified something earlier in the conversation which had upset him. I hadn't attended to it. Before we parted we cleared the matter between us. Our friendship is deeper than ever.

EXPLORING YOUR RELATIONSHIPS
Two Boats

To get the most out of this phantasy, put yourself in a quiet place where you are not likely to be disturbed. Make yourself comfortable, loosening any tight clothing and removing your glasses. When you are settled and at ease, take three or four deep, deep breaths. Breathe in slowly, hold it, breathe out slowly. Then breathe at a restful rate. Keep your attention on your breathing.

Imagine yourself in the middle of a lake on a lovely summer day. The sky is blue. Calm lake water reflects the blue sky. There is a light breeze. Look at the boat which you are occupying.

What kind of boat is it? Describe it.

Look around the boat. Check it from stem to stern and notice what you have with you. *What is in the boat?*

Remembering that all things are possible in imagination, you gradually become aware that someone is in the boat with you. Let that person come into focus for you. *Who is with you?*

While you are in the boat together, enjoying the lake, you notice that a speedboat is approaching. It comes closer and closer and with great speed.

What do you and the person in the boat with you do?

As you prepare to let the phantasy fade, pay attention to your feeling tone. Now let the phantasy fade and bring yourself consciously back to the room where you are. Sit or stand and stretch a bit. Then you are ready to think or talk about your phantasy. ⊶⟶⊷

For this phantasy, let's take it one question at a time.

What kind of boat did you see?

People told me they were in rowboats. Rowboats are sturdy, plain, little, "tested for seaworthiness" before going out, simple, as people described them. Some were in skiboats (one called hers "new and shiny, with a lovely sun deck"). Others found themselves in powerful motorboats or graceful, swift sailboats. One woman had a canoe, wondering if it were floatable. A man had an aluminum canoe which changed to a birch canoe as the rest of his phantasy went back in time. Whatever the kind of boat you imagined, pay attention to it and what it might mean for how you see your life at this point. Is it in good repair? Serviceable? Able to convey what it must?

When you checked the boat, what did you find in it?

One man had extra flotation devices, extra flares, extra gas. Plenty of food and drink and a change of clothes were also in the boat. He is a very cautious man, careful that everything is right.

People frequently find their boat containing picnic supplies. They say things like: "an ice chest with goodies"; "a blanket and a bathing suit"; "picnic supplies, sunglasses, a book"; "a six pack and picnic things"; "a bathing suit and a radio." One woman got a little ahead of the rest of us and found "two children and their parents." A Sister discovered "my Bible and a sack lunch." One found "peppermint life savers." For another it was fishing gear. These things show ordinary people expecting a pleasant time.

What did you find? What might that indicate about you?

Who was the person who appeared in the boat with you? Often times it is husband or wife. Sometimes it is mother or father, brother or sister. Friends. A business associate. Someone with whom there is unfinished business. Occasionally a person meets another aspect of himself or herself. Whoever it was, attend to that person and the reason why it is important now.

As the speedboat came closer and closer, what did you and the person with you do?

One man said "rowed like hell and yelled at my wife to save the seat cushions." When I asked him what that showed about his personal style he responded, "I take command in situations. I also am cautious and check things out before I trust."

The lady with the lovely sun deck on her boat continued to laze in the sun. Her friend turned the motor on and got the boat out of the way. ("I like being taken care of," was her comment.)

"My pond was too small for another boat to come along and do much damage," reported one contented phantasizer, "so I waved and kept on eating my lunch."

The children in one boat noticed the speedboat towing a water skier. They concluded the speedboat pilot didn't see them, so they managed to attract his attention. He swerved in time.

Sister was out catching salamanders from her rowboat. She found Jesus as her companion. "He sat there radiating. I didn't catch all he was saying, but I had a sense it was all right." She went on to say that when danger threatened, she still had a sense it was all right, but all Jesus did was go on "radiating" while she had to do the rowing to get out of the way. That she did, just in time. The water from the other boat's wake was turbulent enough to get into her boat. Jesus "kept on radiating" while she bailed. Very enjoyable classical music was playing all the time.

Two brothers were fishing quietly enjoying each other's

company when the threatening speedboat appeared. They yelled, they waved. Nothing caught the other unseen pilot's attention. "My brother and I jumped before the speedboat demolished our small rowboat," the man told me. He and his brother checked each other; both were unhurt. They swam easily to shore.

"What do you make of it?" I asked him. Thoughtfully he answered, "Well, we care about each other, and that's not always easy to say. We survive well, too. Sometimes catastrophe comes, and we can't do much about it, but we survive."

As one man's aluminum canoe suddenly changed to a birch canoe, so did his jeans change to deerskin pants. Animal skins filled his canoe—results of his trapping expedition. He had nothing else, but knew he could take care of himself in the forest. Another aspect of himself appeared in the boat—his *anima*. They continued their usual bickering and struggle for acceptance. When the speedboat came bearing down on them, he said he'd save her if she fell overboard. If the reverse were true, would she come back for him? He thought so, but wasn't sure. As it turned out both survived the bumping wake of the careless speedboat. The radio played a duet of male and female voices.

A canoeist and her friend had cushions and lifesavers in the craft. When the speedboat came near they both jumped, hanging on to the lifesavers. She didn't notice if the canoe were hit or not.

A man and his sister were in the rowboat enjoying the sun after a swim. When the speedboat approached he wanted to jump; she persuaded him to wait. The speedboat came right up to their smaller boat. There was an urgent message for the man to go ashore and call his wife.

It is useful to mull over what you did when the speedboat came toward you. Did you expect harm? Were you naive? What steps did you take? Did others help? How did you act in times of emergency? How do you care for yourself? For other people? And how do you feel about it later?

With whatever insights come from this you are in a better position to make decisions about your own behavior.

EXPLORING YOUR RELATIONSHIPS

Toys

Take the time to stretch, and then make yourself comfortable. Either sit or lie down, remove your shoes and glasses, loosen any clothing which might be tight.

Take several slow, deep breaths. Attend only to your breathing. Now breathe more slowly and at an even pace. When other thoughts come, acknowledge them and gently let them go. Think only of your breathing.

Imagine yourself entering a large old–fashioned house. Go through the pleasant entry hall, and up the broad, carpeted stairs to a large bedroom. Obviously it is a child's room, and there are many toys.

As you look around the room, you gradually realize you are a toy. *What kind of toy are you?*

Look at the toy you are. Examine it. Really notice things about you.

Now find another toy. *What other toy comes to you?*

What is that toy like?

You and the other toy have an exchange, an encounter. *What happens between you?*

You begin to notice that the other toys are watching the two of you, and the others are talking among themselves. *What are the other toys saying about you?*

Let the phantasy fade. Come back to this room, this place. As you are ready, sit up. Stretch and yawn if you like.

Begin thinking or talking about this phantasy.

When doing this phantasy people often revert to their own childhood toys. That's fine. Sometimes they are toys they never had, or even remember ever seeing. That's fine, too. When the other toy is a multiple toy (a game with parts, a ball and jacks, a set of things), generally it means that it is not another person, but a group (family, community, work group) with whom the interaction is taking place.

What the other toys are saying indicates how others respond to the relationship in the first part of the phantasy. Perhaps a few examples will help clarify this.

A woman said she was a teddy bear. A large and very pretty doll came to join her. The doll brushed the teddy's fur, petted her, and swung her round and round in the air. The teddy bear was a bit embarrassed that she didn't give the doll much, but she enjoyed the attention and the play. However, the other toys were disapproving and were saying, "You're too big to be doing that." Their disapproval didn't stop her, although she wondered why they were so cross.

Similar to that phantasy was a man's who was also a teddy bear. A clay duck on wheels with a long string embraced him. They enjoy a good friendship. The other toys in his phantasy were divided. Some thought it was good that they were friends; others disapproved. At first this man said they didn't understand. Then he acknowledged their lack of understanding (or jealousy) really hurt him.

Another man was a pinball machine. A toy firetruck came over to him, raised its ladder, and they had a fine time watching the scene in the playroom. Raggedy Ann and Andy were dancing and the other toys singing and clapping to keep time. He felt very much a part of it.

A woman was a rag doll. She found herself unable to speak to the drummer who came to her, but bowed and was glad to see him. He showed he was glad to be with her by beating his drum as he marched in circles around her. They were having a fine time. The other toys complained that they were making too much noise. That hurt the rag doll, but didn't stop her bowing or the drummer's drumming.

The man was a puppet; the other toy was also a puppet. They danced but with no gladness. Other toys kept saying, "We don't like the puppet master, either."

"I was a ballerina, spinning on my toes," said a lady. "The other toy was a wooden soldier. He kept sticking out his long gun, trying to trip me. But the other toys shouted to me to go on dancing." She was encouraged to deal more directly with the wooden soldier in her life.

Another person was a chunky, built–close–to–the–ground gold and blue striped top—the kind with a string to yank and music to play. A hard little red ball and a set of jacks came over to her. The ball and jacks taunted her, "We are made for big kids. You're just for a baby." The woman who was the top felt inferior and competitive at the same time. When the other toys looked over the situation, their judgment was, "We need both. There are all sizes of kids in the world." At those words the top felt fine both with herself and with the ball and jacks.

"I became a zippered–up dog . . . the kind whose mouth opens wide; you can put things in and then zip open his back to remove them. I thought it was a kind of interesting toy to be." The other toy was a floppy pink doll with long eyelashes. The floppy pink doll snuggled up to the dog and rested there. None of the other toys except a big swing said anything. Said the swing to the snuggling pair, "You can come and sit on me." It was a good and welcoming feeling for the zippered–up dog.

A man saw himself as a toy soldier, with crossed white bands on his chest and very shiny shoes. The other toy was lots of toy wooden soldiers, all dressed like himself. They were playing at derailing the toy train. None of the other toys would talk to them.

This phantasy can serve a double purpose. Sometimes the other toy is a person quite significant in your life. Your relationship is shown by the kind of toys in relationship and the interaction between them (toy soldiers wrecking toy trains; toy soldier trying to trip up the ballerina; the doll brushing and petting and swinging the teddy bear).

What the other toys are saying is sometimes a source of insight. ("We need both. There are kids of all sizes in the world," relieved the inferior feelings of the top.) Sometimes what they are saying shows others' reactions to a given relationship. The phantasy can be affirmative ("Come sit on me," said the swing) or negative ("You're too big for that"). It can surface jealousy and hurts that might be hidden under "They just don't understand . . . It's all right" statements made easily, but which DO NOT help us at all.

Reconciliation

This phantasy has a very special meaning for me. I offer it here because I think that in the lives of all of us, there comes a time when we are treated insultingly. As a result we are angry at the unfairness of it; hurt that it "happened to me"; afraid that maybe the other person is right; resentful, especially if the perceived insult were given publicly.

This phantasy has a special meaning to me because of the first time I used it. I was with a group of people at a meeting. They are people I really care for and like very much. One of the speakers who was well enough prepared did not understand the audience. Nor they, him. By the end of the day, there was a pervasive atmosphere of depression, upset, anger, wanting to "escape." But all of the people involved were good people. I counted on that. This phantasy was done with them. Any one of us might find it useful in a hurtful situation. If you, now, are seething and smarting from some hurt, you will probably find it more difficult to relax. Do a few minutes of physical exercise. Stretch, reach for your toes, bend to the right and to the left slowly. (And don't forget to breathe.) Clasp your hands in front of your chest and turn to the right as far as you can; then, slowly to the left as far as you can. Roll your head around a few times to the right; to the left. Repeat these motions.

Dim the room. If any sound system is on, turn it off, making the room as quiet as you can. Remove your shoes, your glasses. Lie down if it is convenient. Sitting or lying, tense all of your muscles. Make your whole body as tight as you can. Hold it tense for a few seconds. Now, let go. If you want to make a noise exhaling, do so. Let go some more. Feel yourself sinking into the bed, or floor, or chair. Breathe normally and naturally, attending to your breathing. If thoughts or strong feelings persist in coming, let them. Acknowledge them and gently let them go. Pay attention only to your breathing.

Now imagine yourself in an open space. By your side is a large pile of plastic garbage bags and a package of ties for them. It's a good size pile. Notice them. Know that they are yours, there for your use. ⊶———⊷

Now, slowly—very slowly—go back through the dismaying incident. Go back over the day, the time when these unpleasant, these ugly, things took place. Isolate the grievances bit by bit. Put each one separately into a garbage bag and tie it securely. Set that bag aside and fill another one. Take your time. ⊶———⊷

Are you sure you have everything that happened garbage–bagged? Take a few more moments. Did you bag the words? the sound of the voice? the gestures? laughter? the sarcasm or ridicule? Did you get everything? Take as much time as you want. There are plenty of bags and ties. Use all you want. ⊶———⊷

When you are satisfied that everything from that difficult situation is in a garbage bag, stand back and look at the cluster of them. (If you think of another thing, that's all right. Add it to the pile.) Just look at them for a few moments. ⊶———⊷

Walk slowly toward the group of bags. You don't have to think or reason, just walk slowly toward them, and around them. One of the bags (it doesn't matter which one, or why) will attract you. Let your hand reach out and take that bag. Wait for it to attract you. Then remove it from the pile. ⊶———⊷

Walk a little apart. Open the bag. Remove the contents. Spill them out on the ground. Look at them. Look at what came out of that bag. ⊶———⊷

Pick up the contents of that bag. Hold them. Something changes. *What changes?*

Pay attention to the change and what it means to you. *How do you feel?* Pay attention to that, too.

Let the phantasy fade. Become conscious of this present time, this room. You might well like to stretch again, and yawn. When you are ready begin to go over the phantasy.

People react to the garbage bags differently. Some stuff them with a vengeance, delighted with the physical activity and with getting the dismal stuff out of sight. Some seem reluctant to get started—they feel inclined to bury the day whole. (It is much more useful, in my experience, to take care of it piece by piece at this point.) Others are quite methodical, accounting carefully for every bit of the situation. Still others are somewhat chaotic. It's almost as if they were saying, "There was this ____! And this ____! And would you believe, ____! Worst of all, ____! I almost forgot ____!"

How did you fill your bags? It is important that you did bag all of that situation. What might also be an insight into yourself is how you go about things like this. *How did you go about the task?*

Then you stood back and looked at it. It's good to get a little space and not think precisely about each part. Walking toward and around the bags gives you time to let one attract you. You need not explain nor defend the attraction. It just is there.

When you picked up one bag, took it apart, opened it, and removed the contents, *what were they?*

When you picked the contents up and held them, *what happened?*

And what difference did it make?

Before I tell you how some other people responded to this phantasy I need to tell you something else. All of the people in the group had done the God tree phantasy. That affected several of them.

When one man spilled his bag's contents on the ground, all of the hurts and insults he had felt had solidified into a large chunk of liver. He found it very hard to pick up—and a bit disgusting as well. But he did so. He felt very sad and found it hard to breathe, holding on to that stuff. So he let it go and slither away. The pain left his chest.

"I put all the things I didn't like about the other person in one very large garbage bag," said one man. "When you said to spill it out on the ground, I felt great. I thought, 'Here's my chance really to stomp it all into the ground.' But all those bad things I had put into the bag didn't come out. They weren't there. What came out was a bunch of roses! I didn't know what to do with them, so I put them in front of my God tree." What changed for him was that now he could reach his God tree. In the prior phantasy he couldn't do that.

This man's experience is not very unusual. Between the time we put things into the garbage bag and take them out, they sometimes change.

A similar thing happened to another person in the group. When he went to empty his bag of uglies, the "father of the prodigal son came out. So I dumped him gently on the ground, then took his hand, raised him up and we embraced." He added, "I guess what changed is me."

One of the bags was full of white and gray boxes. The

owner took them, threw them into a fire, and "felt great!"

When the bag was selected out of the group by another person, the sky darkened with heavy storm clouds. The bag was very heavy and caused fear in its owner. Shock, surprise, and fear were its original contents. They were still there. What could be done? The idea that he could do something surprised this person. When he realized he wasn't powerless, there was no hesitation. He took it spontaneously to his God tree and opened it there. There he felt safe and he began to understand the neediness of the one who had offended him. "When I became aware of this, a feeling of peace and content—and even accomplishment—came over me. Then I looked out over the countryside again and the storm clouds were no more."

All of the bad things for another person were still in the bag when it was opened. At first the thought came, "They are so stinky they'd make good fertilizer!" Then the thought came, "I don't want them in *my* yard!" So the stinky things were thrown away. What changed? "That was funny. I went back to the other phantasy and *my tree* had grown!"

One last example. Again, bags were full of miserable things. What had happened and the bad memories they had provoked were there. When the contents were spilled out on the ground they had changed into the person's own memories of when a similar thing had happened to him. He was overcome with sympathy and understanding. He picked up the understandings, embraced them and felt very much at one with the other person.

What happened in each of these instances is, I think, very beautiful. Each one involved did not deny the hurt, the feelings of outrage, insult, hostility. Those feelings were looked at and put into bags. One—for whatever reason (certainly very particular to each person)—attracted the person. In some way (burned, thrown away, put down before God, embraced) the uglies were let go. No one held on to them, wallowed in them, fed them. The people let go. And in letting go, by whatever means, they themselves were freed. Many reported that the tension headaches, backaches, stiff necks, queasy stomachs experienced prior to this exercise disappeared. There was real tranquillity in the room by the end of the evening.

Farewell

Find a nice quiet place. Either dim the light or draw the blinds. Make yourself comfortable, having removed shoes, glasses and loosened tight clothing.

Breathe slowly and deeply for several breaths. Now let the cares of the day flow through and out of you. Breathe regularly and attend to your breathing. When you are quiet begin the phantasy.

You are having a grand vacation. Island–hopping is something you might not have done before, but you find it very agreeable. You are on a large pleasure ship in the Carribean. There isn't a care in your world. You are well taken care of and enjoying yourself immensely.

At the moment you have just reboarded the ship after an island stop. The next island is only a few hours away. Just before the gangplank is lifted a new passenger comes aboard. It's someone you know. Someone you are very surprised to see. *Who comes aboard?*

You meet the person, and you agree to spend some time together. An inexorable conviction comes over you that you will never see this person again. You *know* you will not meet again. *What do you talk about?*

There isn't much time left. One of you turns to the other and with the utmost seriousness says, "What I really want you to know is. . . ." *What is it?*

The ship is about ready to dock. You and the other person have to take leave of each other. Bid each other farewell.

Let the phantasy fade. As you are ready, come back to this room, this time and place. Let's go through it.

"Farewell" is an emotionally difficult phantasy. Knowing it is the last chance to speak with the other person lends a poignancy and anxiety to it that affects people very deeply. What is significant to you in the relationship is just about bound to surface. And what is significant frequently is unfinished business. ⊶——⊸

Often the person who crosses the gangplank is unexpected. For one woman it was an old friend with whom the friendship had taken a turn into animosity. Still she cared about her former friend. On shipboard she asked the other person serious questions concerning her feelings and attitudes toward matters of mutual concern. She insisted on serious answers, not the flippant ones which had become current. She got them. What emerged was that there was an encrusted but still real concern between them which was mutual.

For a man it was an unwelcome ex–girl friend who came aboard. Well, she was "ex" for him, but she was still pursuing the relationship. Right behind her was another friend, a man whom he deeply respected but hadn't seen in years. The three of them went to an upper deck. There the phantasizer walked round and round the deck with his male friend. "There just was nothing left to say to the girl," he reported. Then he thought how well his male friend could care for the girl. Yet when they left ship, she went one way, he another. Peace was the predominant feeling. He had really said good–bye to her. So he went back to the upper deck and ordered a Bloody Mary.

For another person, the man who came aboard was just a casual acquaintance. While their relationship was not significant, what had happened between them was disturbing. During the phantasy they talked about the unpleasant incident. Each said how each perceived it. Both had misread the situation and therefore had acted inappropriately. For the one having the phantasy, there was an experience of forgiveness and tranquillity.

In the family of one person, there is a young girl who has left home with anger and bitterness. This woman saw her niece come aboard. The girl spoke readily to her aunt. Insisting her parents would never understand and would never accept her, she refused to go home. At least they talked, but seemingly to no avail. The woman was left with much sadness.

A married man saw a much loved woman, not his wife, unexpectedly come aboard. They met. Their love for each other still is strong; their commitment to other people still is strong. Talking about the ordinary, everyday things of their lives on a sun deck they enjoyed each other's company with both longing and respect. When the ship docked they embraced wordlessly and parted.

The purpose of this phantasy is to examine either a significant relationship or an incident of some importance. Often what emerges is unfinished business.

In the course of human living, people grow apart for a variety of reasons. Resentment, anger, and jealousy get mixed up with the love, affection, and pleasure of each other's company. In a phantasy of this sort the deeper, truer underlying attitude will surface. In one of the responses given above, the "ex" girl friend truly was "ex" for the man—the phantasy reaffirmed that the relationship was over for him, if not for her. For the first woman the friendship–turned–flippant showed itself as still having depth. She intends to pursue it in a visit to her friend. When the phantasy leads to changed behavior (as the intended visit to take care of unfinished business), it serves its intended purpose.

Three Boxes

Life is full of choices. Often enough the choices I am facing are not between good and evil, but between two good things. Even then which is better is not clear. Pros and cons are on both sides. I talk about it with people, I think and pray about it, and still I don't know what I am going to do. Faced with the problem of making a choice among good alternatives, I need something to help me make up my mind. This phantasy can serve the purpose.

Find a quiet place and make yourself comfortable. Take several deep breaths slowly, consciously. Then breathe regularly, paying attention only to your breathing. As other thoughts come acknowledge them, knowing you will take care of them later, then let them go.

When you are quiet, imagine three boxes.

What do the boxes look like? . . . What size are they?

Look at them and notice the one to your left, the one in the middle, and the one to your right. Approach one of the boxes.

Which one attracted you? Look at it, then open it. *What do you find inside?*

Does anything happen?

Go to another box. Which one do you approach? Open it. *What do you find inside? Does anything happen?*

Now go to the remaining box. Open this one, too. You find something inside of it. *What do you find? Does anything happen?*

Take the three things that you have found and look at them. Perhaps there is some interaction among them. If so, notice it. ⋈⋆────⋆⋈

Let the phantasy fade. Sit or stand up and stretch. You might want to yawn.

Go over the phantasy when you are alert. You may do it alone, or you may want to talk it over with someone else.

Go back to the beginning of the phantasy. Which box did you go to first? If you are righthanded and you went to the one on the right side you are likely to be rather defensive (or, if you are lefthanded and went to the one on the left). If you went to the one on the opposite side (left side for a righthanded person) then you were probably quite free and open to the phantasy. If you chose the box in the middle you tend to favor a safe position.

What did you find? What might that mean to you?

One woman first found a lovely spring hat. In her second box was a Bible. And in the third, a diamond. She said she likes beautiful things, perhaps to the point of letting them influence her life more than she really wants. The Bible reminded her to keep things in perspective according to where she is going.

Another person found a fire hydrant in her first box. A plain old fire hydrant. In the second box was a doll carriage, empty save for a doll's blanket and pillow. In the third box was a puppy, and evidence that the puppy had been in the box a while. The puppy jumped into the lap of the person having the phantasy, then got up and used the fire hydrant. She said if she decided to stay where she was, it was safe and sound, and she was as needed as a fire hydrant. Yet, the only box that contained life was the last one she opened. It was a new life (a puppy). What was the message for the safe and sound present? The decision was to move.

Old photos of home were in the first box. Old letters from home were in the second box. The third box was empty. With tears this person said things really needed to be sorted out. A visit with the family members in this country was planned.

A man had big, strong boxes. Straw was in the first one; the second was empty. Out of the third came a shiny, lively ball. Wherever he went the ball was with him as a kind of fun companion. He delighted in its presence. The man said he is moving to an important new job in a few months and this phantasy reassured him that his was a good decision.

A young woman found a cement bucket full of brilliant fuschias in her first box. In the second she saw a snake. As she hesitantly reached toward it, it disappeared and a very good friend came out of the box. A small country church was in the third. She and her friend visited the church and then shared important things going on in their lives. This woman laughed ruefully at herself. She said she often thinks good things can't last, so she couldn't find something good in the second box. But when she stayed with it the reality was that it was very good indeed.

The Island

To get the most out of this phantasy, put yourself in a quiet place where you are not likely to be disturbed. Make yourself comfortable, loosening any tight clothing and removing your glasses and shoes. Stretch. Yawn. When you are settled and at ease take three or four deep, deep breaths. Breathe in slowly; hold each breath for a count of five; breathe out slowly. Then breathe at a restful rate. If other thoughts come, acknowledge them; then gently let them go. Keep your attention on your breathing.

Imagine yourself in the middle of a lake on a lovely summer day. The sky is blue. Calm lake water reflects the blue sky. There is a light breeze. Look at the boat you are occupying.
What kind of boat is it? Describe it.

Look around the boat. Check it from stem to stern and notice what you have with you. *What is in the boat?*

You are alone in the boat. The day is very enjoyable for you.

Gradually you become aware the sun isn't so warm as it was; the breeze isn't so gentle as it was. In fact, the wind is rising and heavy clouds are rolling. The water is becoming quite choppy.

As a storm approaches you begin to be quite apprehensive. You prepare to bring the boat to shore. ⊶⟶⟝⊸

The wind and water are proving too much for you and your craft. Fortunately, there is an island between you and the shore and you head for it. Get yourself there. ⊶⟶⟝⊸

The storm is raging. You are on the island. *What do you do?*

By the time the storm is over it is almost nighttime. You walk along the shore of the island and look over the lake. Another boat is out there. In fact, it is heading right toward the island. You watch it approach, then come into shore, beaching right in front of you. *Who is in it?*

What happens with that person?

Let the phantasy fade. Become aware of this time, this place. After you have stretched (and perhaps put your glasses back on) think or talk about the phantasy.

Let's review this phantasy, too, bit by bit.

When the storm started to come, how did you react? With how much difficulty did you reach the island? Were you sure of your own ability?

One man said that he had a sailboat and it was a pleasure to bring it in—the wind was just right. Another person's motor kept missing and she prayed a lot. Finally the motor caught and she arrived safely. A boy's boat sprung a leak, and between trying to bail it out enough to keep it afloat and row enough to get to shore he became exhausted and abandoned it.

He swam into the beach. Some people come in with comparative ease ("I just gunned the engine and raced in," said one). Others have more trouble from the start, when they hit the surf, they beach the craft. It's important to note whether your boat supported you or if it failed you. Did you stay with it or leave it? And why? How does that fit in with the way you generally react in troubled times?

What did you do when you reached the island?

Some people explore. They find shelter on the island, or materials with which to shelter themselves from the storm. Others find nothing. Some find helpful natives. Others find hostile people—either strangers or people in their lives from whom they expect bad treatment. What you found indicates your expectations when in need. What you did indicates your perception of your own resourcefulness. For instance, some build a shelter from materials found in the woods. Some merely turn their boat upside down, wrap up in a blanket and munch a lunch while waiting out the storm. Some even enjoy the storm from whatever place they find or make. Others are wretched; attacked by hostile nature, bugs, animals and occasionally, by people. What did you do? What do you infer from this? You might want to check your perception of your behavior with someone who will respond honestly to you.

The storm was over. What was it like when you walked on the beach? Was it a mess, full of debris? Was your boat wrecked? Was it serviceable? Was it a pretty sight? What was it like for you?

A boat appears and comes to shore. How did you feel when you saw it?

Some people are again expecting some harm to come to them. Others are relieved, thinking they will be rescued. Occasionally someone is annoyed—either at the interruption of the welcome solitude just enjoyed, or at being too well taken care of. A man who had a sleek sailboat had a very good time by himself on the island. His sailboat had been damaged and he had just begun repairing it while singing at the top of his lungs. When a large powerboat appeared he *knew* it would be his wife. It was. On the other hand, in her phantasy, his wife had a powerboat which was also damaged.

When she walked along the shore after the storm had abated she saw a sailboat and *knew* her husband would be in it. He was, and after seeing she was unharmed, he suggested they leave the powerboat there and that she join him in the sailboat. She said she did—even though she does not like sailboats. When this couple exchanged phantasies they were a little embarrassed, a little amused, and very pleased with themselves and each other.

Who was in the boat which came to your shore? What happened? Most importantly, what does it mean to you in your expectations of people? If the person in the other boat was someone known to you (not shore patrol or a stranger), what insight might you have into this relationship?

Surprise

As you are about ready to engage in this phantasy, take the time to make yourself comfortable. Turn off the television or radio. Remove your glasses, and shoes too, if you wish. Loosen any tight clothing.

Now take a few deep breaths. Breathe in to a slow count of five, hold it for a slow count of five, and exhale to a slow count of five. Do this three or four times.

Breathe regularly now, attending only to your breathing.

Imagine yourself on a beach. Look around you. What kind of day is it? Which season? What is the weather like? How does the water seem?

Look up and down the beach. What do you see? Are there any other people in sight? If so, what are they doing?

Start walking. You are rather carefree and enjoying yourself on the beach.

In the distance you see something on the beach. You are a bit curious as you walk toward it. You are nearly there now. It is a chest, partially submerged in the sand. The water has receded and as you tug at the chest you find that it moves rather easily. Pull the chest out of the sand and move it a bit further up the beach. You are able to do this readily.

The lid is closed but not locked. You raise the lid and look inside. *What do you find?*

Take it out and examine it carefully. *What do you experience?*

Somehow you know that this is not for you to keep. When you are ready, put what you have found back into the box. Close the lid. Start retracing your steps down the beach. Be aware of how you are feeling. ⊶⊶

Let the phantasy fade. Bring yourself back to the present moment, to this room. When you are ready, sit or stand, stretch, perhaps yawn.

Now you are ready to think about or talk about your phantasy.

Which of the seasons emerged for you? When "beach" is mentioned, many people think summer. That is when most of their beach–going is enjoyed. But that's not always so. Whatever the season, what might that season mean to you?

Combined with the weather, what does that mean to you? Remember Rule #3. Bleak winter days and storms may mean a bleak time in life with stormy encounters. It also could recall a fun time when you were with friends and had an adventurous day on the beach. Or a day when things became clear and you made a significant decision. Whatever it was, attend to the season and the weather and muse a while. What do they signify for you?

When you looked up and down the beach, what did you see? Clear, clean shore? Debris? People? Seagulls? A dog? It could be that your memory was coming into play and you saw a real scene. That is all right. Is it a memory? Does it have any particular affective meaning for you? Was it something different (although the parts come from memory)? How did you feel as you looked up and down the beach? Lonely? Forsaken? Serene? Glad for the space? Annoyed at the crowds, their radios and noise? Forsaken, with no one in sight? Relieved at being alone and enjoying it? Amused at the sandpipers or fishing gulls? Interested in the fishing boats? How did you respond to the situation?

When you came upon the chest, how did that affect you? Were you apprehensive or hesitant about moving and opening it? Feeling adventurous, perhaps a bit excited? Bored? Interested? Did anyone see you? Did it make any difference that you were alone—or that someone else was there?

Looking at your answers to these questions, ask yourself, *what might this tell me about my usual attitude when facing something a bit uncertain?*

What did you find in the chest? What was it like? How did you examine it? With what results?

Most important of all: *what does what you found mean to you?*

How did you respond to the suggestion to return it to the chest and leave?

One young woman found herself striding briskly on the beach on a bright autumn day. Scarlet and gold–leaved trees were in sight further inland; but the sand, warmed by the sun, felt good under her feet. She found a gold chain in the chest. It had a many–faceted jewel pendant. After turning it this way and that in the sun and admiring its sparkling beauty, she put it on. "I just felt very happy, sitting alone on the beach and looking at the shining beauty of the water and of my pendant. It reminded me of how rich my life is in the things that count to me." When asked to return it to the chest she said she "felt sad, and at first did not want to do it." Then she realized that the pendant was meant for many people to enjoy. She returned it and walked away still feeling rich.

A science teacher never got to open the chest. He had no

trouble approaching it on his fine summer day. When he got close he found the chest partially submerged in the sand right next to an unexpected tidal basin. This teacher forgot the chest and its possible contents. He plopped on his stomach and spent the time happily gazing into the clear water at the shells, rocks and life teeming in the pool. He reported himself utterly delighted with his find.

The day was chilly and gloomy. Rain fell lightly. "I thought I might find a raincoat or blanket in the chest," said my friend, "but what was there was a big flashlight. I took it out and laughed. Whenever things are gloomy, a light comes eventually. I put the flashlight back and left grinning. I like walking in the rain."

Another person found herself rather bleakly alone on a rather bleak and debris–laden beach. In the rotting chest she found a chambered nautilus. While looking at it, she said she was mulling over how her past and present affect each other.

One lady said she was strolling by herself on a sort of nondescript day. She wasn't particularly feeling anything. In the whole big chest what she discovered was one joined sea–shell. When she picked it up—rather indifferently—it opened easily. Inside were six pearls. She felt an inexplicable glow of love. "How many children have you?" I asked her. "OH!" Her eyes, her mouth, her whole face smiled. "Four . . . and my husband . . . and myself."

Tomorrow

If possible find a quiet room with dimmed lighting. Make yourself as comfortable as you can (without falling asleep, of course!). Remove your glasses and, if you wish, your shoes. Loosen your belt if it's tight. Take a few deep breaths slowly. Then breathe rhythmically, attending to your breathing. If other thoughts come, allow them, then set them aside gently. Continue slow, steady breathing.

Imagine yourself in the country. It is your favorite time of the year. The weather is perfectly suited to your taste and your mood. Look around and enjoy it.

You are altogether at ease alone in this place. It might be a place familiar to you from your childhood or some other time during your life, or it might be a place new to you. In either case, you are quite comfortable. Now you begin to take a walk. Do so, noticing the country around you.

Not far in the distance you see a house. Somehow you feel drawn to it. Walk toward it.

As you come up to the house you are only faintly surprised to find your name on the mailbox. There's no mail—not even a paper. But this does not surprise you, either. You go up the walk to the front door and into the house. Explore your house.

Somewhere inside that house you will find a door with your name over it. Look for that door.

Under your name there is one other word: TOMORROW. You look at it, and then go into the room. In a very special way, more than all the rest of the house, this room is yours. Take your time and examine the room carefully.

Even though you have looked around the room carefully,

there is one item you perhaps have not noticed. Over in a corner, or maybe against a wall, is a box. Find the box. ⊶——•⊷

The box has a label. It says HINDRANCES. You know the box contains hindrances to your tomorrow. Open the box and pay very careful attention to its contents. ⊶——•⊷

Do something with the contents of the box. ⊶——•⊷

Now leave the room that is yours. Leave the house. Go back down the pathway, through the woods and return to where you began this journey. ⊶——•⊷

Let the phantasy fade. Come back to this time, this place. Sit up. You may want to stretch.

Now begin to think or talk about your phantasy.

What were the season and weather like for you? What special meaning has it for you that it has become your favorite season?

People vary a good deal on this. Some enjoy summer best. They find it most pleasant and remember vacation times, or perhaps a vacation house. Some like the fall, with its bright foliage and brisk days, the smell of burning leaves, the remembrance of school and games or perhaps family get–togethers at Thanksgiving. Winter sports enthusiasts find snow, and perhaps ski slopes. One person's house was all ready for Christmas. Spring, with budding trees and flowers—even sun showers and walking in the rain—is a common choice. New life and the joy of the season, perhaps a wedding anniversary, triggers it off. Birthdays, anniversaries, and special family memories are often behind favorite seasons and weather. What was yours?

What was your house like? Large? Small? Modest? Ordinary? Grand? Pretentious? Well–kept? In disrepair? Lonely? Neglected? Welcoming? Just there? How did your house impact you when you saw it?

One man saw a sturdy cabin; another, a three–storied white house with columns. Some find brick or stone. A woman saw a handmade wooden house, with many fine, hand–crafted details. How did you feel about the house you found?

And what was it like inside for you? One woman reported

hers had lovely, but faded, wallpaper. It felt like it had enclosed some happy times, but it was all in the past. That was so until she found her room. A man found all sorts of interesting things in his house, but they were all in glass cases (to be seen, not touched). Many just enjoy walking around their house. Some find it repugnant and unhappy, with debris and broken furniture cluttering the rooms. Others are rather neutral about the whole thing. Many experience it as pleasant.

There's a room with your name on it. Under your name is one other word: TOMORROW. That is done for the purpose of planning for the immediate future. Not five–or–ten–year plans, but a simple change possible for tomorrow.

The room is yours. People find bedrooms and can describe them well. Small, but the window has a good view. Medium, and wall–to–wall carpeting. An all wood floor: most of the floor is oak with an intricate design. The center is plain pine. (That man has a soft heart.) Some people find "their room" to be a living room. One woman's "own" living room had centers in it: for conversation, for games, for reading. These phantasized living rooms frequently are very welcoming. Some are very well cared for (everything protected by plastic and somewhat inaccessible to human comfort) in a way that gives the impression things are more important than people. Living rooms can be cluttered, comfortable, in disarray, barren.

An office or a study is the named room for others. A woman had a very functional office, but there were plants flourishing on top of the file cabinets. The father of a young family saw a study, with floor–to–ceiling bookshelves, well–filled, comfortable, and "out of bounds" to his lively toddlers. Another woman saw her childhood playroom which brought back long–forgotten memories.

In the room, you found a box labeled HINDRANCES. Suggesting hindrances, and allowing them to emerge imaginatively, permits consideration of an area requiring change.

All sorts of boxes are found. Big wooden ones. Cardboard dress boxes. Crates. Treasure chests. Empty liquor cartons. Egg boxes. Grocery store cartons. Some are covered and locked. Others have no cover. Most people don't have trouble opening the box. A few do. Resistances and fears become evident in a variety of ways. However, almost everyone does manage to open the box. The kind of box may itself have meaning. How well–protected are the hindrances? And how treasured?

What is inside the box? I find that people's discoveries mainly go one of two ways. Some find things that indicate blatantly what the obstacle in their life is, or things symbolic of the obstacle. Others find some kind of "notice" of what is hindering their living well.

For instance, one woman's box contained "shyness." She just knew it was "shyness." Another found "always worrying things won't turn out well." A man talked about his finding "inability to accept the weirdos in his life." For someone else it was "a combination of fear and awe" at a time when a new job contract had just been signed.

A good number of people find things. A woman found a broken watch. She talked about how poorly she handles time and the effect that has in her life and in her relationships. Another person, currently in an unhappy (although self–chosen) situation, found an eye which she promptly threw out the window. She didn't want to see the implications of her choice. A man was startled by opening the box and finding his own face reflected in the mirror there. Another person had a box full of masks. Thoughtfully he talked about being more honest with people. Someone else found glasses. "What might that mean?" I asked. She answered how she hates wearing glasses, how unfree and how irritable they make her feel. A somewhat indolent person found himself in the box, lazily enjoying a hammock. A bottle opener was in another man's box. He decided to discard it and cut down on his drinking. One man found an opened envelope. Try as he would to read it, the "letter" inside was blank. Finally he concluded "I guess I make a big deal out of things that are not that important."

Whatever was in your box—symbol, things, "knowing" something—I'd encourage you to look at it carefully. Let its meaning come to you and make some appropriate decisions from it. Like the man who found his room in disarray. Normally he is moderately neat. In his box were toys. He took them out of the box and put them around the messy and somewhat barren room. "How did that make you feel?" I asked him. "More secure," was his answer. After a moment's quiet he added that he was facing a new job, he didn't feel "together" about it, but he does have things in his past history which give him security and the courage to tackle it.

What about the contents of your box? Your decision?

Part III
SPIRITUAL DIRECTION & PHANTASY

Spiritual Direction
& Phantasy

There is a hunger in this land. The people of these United States are crying the human cry loudly and clearly: "I'm here! . . . Why?"

"I want my life to count."

"I want my time on earth to mean something."

"I want not just to put in time, but quality time."

"I want more—more than consumerism and the economic system can produce."

"I have everything a person could want—good job, good family—and still I'm not satisfied."

"Is that all there is?"

Reactions to the feeling of emptiness vary. Some people seem to settle in and "make do" with more and more of the same: a good education, good job, good house, good car, maybe a boat. They see and are seen in the right places by the right people, doing the right things, behaving the right way. They can be found in an exclusive country club, a church or school society, at the "Y," a local bar, or a laundromat. Many of them are people who feel caught, trapped, empty. They "make do" with the same situation, doing the same things, in the same way, hoping life will turn out differently.

It never does.

"Is that all there is?"

At times like that I'm reminded of John 10:10. Jesus said: "I have come to bring life, and life to the fullest." If Jesus is to be taken seriously, what might that statement mean? In my life? In yours? What is "life to the fullest?" Or, as another translation has it, "life more abundant?"

There's a hunger in the people in this land. People experience what they were told (and believed) is "the good life." Good it is—but not good enough.

The spirit in each of us demands more.

111

"I want deeper relationships with other people."

"I want really to give myself in love. And for someone to love me."

"I want to know God better."

"God's not there anymore."

"Help me with my prayer?"

"I cannot forgive—*that*. How can I say the Lord's prayer?"

"Help me sort out my values—how do I live at home and in the work world and not be torn apart?"

"I pray and pray—and nothing happens. What's wrong?"

"How do I choose to live when each option is a good one?"

"How do I respond to my friends saying, 'You have to live, you know.' "

Yes, I have to live. I want to live well, honestly, with integrity and peace. I want that for myself, my family, my community. Do you find yourself wanting these things too?

These days people are worried about lots of things: health, finances, security, education, safety, work. Yet they long for more and are aware of their longing, their yearning for more.

More what? The appropriate words have been trivalized up front, so let's approach them from behind.

When I feel alone, I want someone with me.

When I feel afraid, I want someone to protect or reassure me.

When I feel happy, I want someone to celebrate with me.

When I am treated badly, I want someone to stand with me.

I don't like it when I feel isolated, separated, abandoned. "Don't like it" isn't strong enough. I get angry at the unfairness; I panic at the fear; I may give up and say I don't care any more. Deep down I know I don't mean it. I do care. I want someone to be with me, to love me—to receive my care and my love.

Isolation, separation, and abandonment are not what I am made for. Union is. Communion and community are—others with me and I with them. Being myself and being with others.

That doesn't mean that I want no solitude. At times I need space and distance, time alone for letting things meld and mix, settle, integrate. Then with renewed strength I can go on.

The trouble is, I know all this. But in my own living I don't always know what to do about it. More than occasionally, I suspect, I'm my own worst barrier to this longed for union with God and other people. I get in my own way. I trip over my own feet—or at least my own untied shoelaces. I have suspected that. Sometimes I have been told that. And I don't know what to do about it.

Then there's this crazy thing that gnaws at me: are other people like me? Or am I crazy? (Maybe I'm only a little crazy, little enough that it doesn't matter much—like when your slip hangs down a little, but at least the lace is pretty and it's clean.) Do other people feel the way I do? Do these thoughts come to them?

How much do people pray, anyway? I don't mean do they go to church regularly (or irregularly—you know how it is!), but do they pray? I don't mean when my wife isn't home, and there's no note or phone call, so I pray, "God, let her be all right." I don't mean when I'm in a hospital waiting room, waiting for the surgeon, praying all the while, "God, please let him get it all. Please. Please." I don't mean, "Please let the phone ring, let a letter come. Please let me get the job, the appointment, the date." In emergencies, of course, people say such things. But what about every day?

Do people pray on ordinary, ho hum days? How do they pray? What happens in their prayer? I know what happens to me. Am I normal? Is my prayer ordinary? I think it's real—is it? Sometimes praying gets so hard that I give up. Is that normal? Why do I feel guilty? Can I be sure about God? It used to seem far easier to "know God's will." Now I wonder if such a thing as God's will really exists. How do I find out? Or am I being silly?

Or are you one who says, "I'm blessed with the kind of faith that says: 'I believe in God'." I believe in God, too. So where do I go from here? How do I deepen my prayer? How do I make progress along the way to fuller union with God? I dearly want to do that. I want to recognize what separates me from God that is my doing. I want to let go of those things in my life that keep us apart. What do I do about the insights I received in the phantasies?

I suppose there are as many questions, as many pleas for help as there are people. In some way or other, the hunger I see in the land comes down to: "I want to be a deeper, fuller, more authentic human being. I want to love the Lord, my God, with my whole heart, soul, and mind, and my neighbor as myself. I want to do that—not just in mere talk, but in my attitudes and behavior—to the core of my being."

That's the hunger.

The question is, "How do I *do* it? *Really* do it?"

The request is, "Please help me."

Clergypersons, people of the Church (however you might define the term) respond to the request quite variously. Some do give the help requested, willingly and well. Others feel embarrassed and incompetent and either repeat unsatisfying platitudes or offer a referral. The hopeful aspect of this situation is that there are more and more people prepared (or preparing) to help each other satisfy the hunger.

Spiritual direction is a traditional term that has been infused with new meanings. No longer is it confined to sacramental ministry or simply combined with the Sacrament of Reconciliation, although that certainly is a legitimate time and place for spiritual direction. Nor is it restricted to an ordained clergy. Today the term can describe the reality of two or more believers meeting each other in a faith context. Nor is the meeting likely to be an authoritarian situation requiring obedience. More than likely it is a meeting of companions on the journey in growth toward God.

Basically, spiritual direction (in the Roman Catholic tradition) involves two or more people. For now, let's consider the usual two, and talk about an alternative later.

One Christian finds the questions, such as those recounted earlier, rising persistently in everyday life. "Here I am! Why? What does it mean?" . . . "How do I make good living the great commandments of loving God with all I am and all I have, and my neighbor as myself?" "How do I learn God's will for me?"

Such a Christian finds another one who is a believer, who is trusted to accept, to understand, to confront, to encourage, and who is judged to be able to give help. The second person responds, "Help?" or "Help!" If both agree to a spiritually directed relationship, it begins and continues in a context of faith—believing in God, believing God, and examining what that means in the ho hum of everyday living as well as in peak or depth moments of decision making, confusion, trouble, joy. Both people are strongly conscious of Eph. 3:20: This relationship *is* the work of the Holy Spirit.

Demands on both sides are serious.

Both must be honest with each other about belief in God— in longing for and searching for union with Him; in Jesus Christ—true God and true man; in Eucharist as central to worship; in Sacred Scripture as the Word of God, to be received and lived; in prayer and in forgiveness as a way of life.

The director (counsellor, guide) needs to be a praying person who has some theological knowledge—especially in spirituality, moral development, and prayer—as well as good insight and perception. Communication skills (especially empathetic listening, confronting, and challenging) are also important. Crucial to spiritual direction is realistic acceptance of the other person as that person IS. Believing in the other and believing the other and believing that there is a deep–down desire—urge—to deepen the relationship with God are essential. Also essential is the willingness to walk with the other person—as long as the other person requests the companionship, and as long as the director judges it useful for the other person. While it is called spiritual direction, and is God–centered, it speaks to the *whole person in the concrete circumstances of life.* No aspect of living is excluded from consideration, since it is the whole person who is baptized and who is yearning for completion in growing toward God.

One help in the process of spiritual direction, for both people involved, is the use of phantasy. As described throughout this book, phantasy is a means to better self–understanding, a tool which can alert the person to previously unattended feelings, motives, behaviors, and attitudes. As such, it is a valuable tool for both the spiritual director and the directee.

The directee (I wish we had a better word!), by asking for

115

this help, is committed to honesty in describing what life in relation to God has been like, where life is now, what kind of life is wanted. Directees make themselves vulnerable. For instance, none of them know what their phantasies might reveal. Willingness to engage in phantasy, for the sake of living the great commandment of love, is one way to make progress. There's nothing magical in the process. The director is not "inspired" with special revelation to tell the other what to do. It's not a command/obey situation. Directees explore alternatives seriously, gain insight, and then make their own decisions. The goal is to act even more freely and lovingly from the depths of the heart. Effort, sustained effort, is required.

There is one large difference between spiritual direction and other forms of counselling. While areas overlap, spiritual direction always involves relationship to God: giving a more wholehearted response to God; developing an increasing awareness of what it means to say we are "created in the image and likeness of God" and made "to be happy forever with Him." The process of spiritual direction involves listening, noticing, and responding to the ways God speaks to us. Very often God speaks through other people. Very often we hear Him through listening to our own deeper selves. Perhaps we need not look so frantically for God; perhaps we ought to be still and let God find us. And when there are encounters with God (however experienced) we need to attend to how the consequences of them might be integrated and lived.

It's a sacred relationship between director and directee—one which necessitates deep respect for the uniqueness of the directee as well as acceptance, sympathy, and patience. It comes by invitation to the core of the directee's living. Look at the questions that the relationship might explore:

"Who is God for you? Who is Jesus for you?"

"How do you experience God?" (Think of your God Tree phantasy.)

"What attracts (or repels) you in Jesus?"

"How do you meet difficulties?" (What did you do in the Cave phantasy? Or in the Hospital one?)

"What do you pray for? . . . How? . . . Then what?"
"How do you forgive? . . . Then what?" (How did the reconciliation phantasy affect you?)

"Look at what you say about God, about prayer, about forgiving: how is that compatible (or incompatible) with the way you live today? Yesterday? . . . What difference will it make tomorrow? Next week?"

The answers looked for are specific, concrete, honest. Or, at least, we work toward such answers. People who have not shared their religious experiences before often have some difficulty articulating them. "I know I feel this way, but I don't know how to say it." "I'm convinced that this is so, but I don't have words for it." At times like these, phantasies can be useful. Sometimes people can't take things head–on. They can take one step to the side and IMAGE how they feel, how they interact.

Some have articulated their love for God, and his for them before—and been ridiculed. "If you're so holy, how come you're still doing *that?*" . . . "You're just trying to impress me, and that won't work!" Once burned, twice shy.

Others have articulated an experience sacred and precious to them and been met with "Oh, yes. Well, as I was saying. . . ." What they valued was dismissed, unattended. Once burned, twice shy.

Some people have experienced excessive admiration. "Gee, I wish I could do that!" "You're wonderful!" In reality, what they want is to examine, explore, and determine the meaning of the experience. Sometimes they just want reassurance. "Yes, that does happen in prayer. Now. . . ."

Most people, I expect, just don't get around to talking much about religious experience, for whatever their network of reasons: fear, shame, embarrassment, anxiety. Someone said that in Victorian times, sexuality was the topic not talked about publicly. Today it's our heartfelt spirituality which is not talked about.

Ideally directees don't look for admiration or for rejection. Matter–of–fact (for it is a matter of fact) acceptance and help are sought. Ideally, directors provide that ministry: simple acceptance; simple belief that the directee is a serious God seeker; simple presence; sometimes not so simple helping.

Initially then, for many people, the questions are, "Where do I find someone who will understand? Whom can I trust? And who has time for me?" These are realistic questions. Frequently they are hard to answer. I'd encourage you, if you are asking them, not to give up. I believe that when we need help, we can generally find it.

Then, "How do I get started? Where do I find the words to describe my deepest longings?"

It's easy to say, "I want to be close to God." Then, what's stopping us?

Nothing's stopping God. He's here, what's in our way? What prevents our living out the inner meaning of our existence?

There are many ways to explore that question. Let's look at prayer as one way.

Who do you know whom you'd call a "prayerful person"? Describe that person in that context. What might your description mean for you?

One of the most prayerful people I know was the librarian of my high school library. Her parents had owned and operated a bar in Brooklyn, New York. Her vocabulary bore traces of her first twenty years on earth. Short–tempered she was and just as quick to laugh at herself; and she was generous. From her it was a challenge, not an irritant, to hear, "What would Jesus do?" It was a challenge because she'd take her own question to heart, and act on it. Or, when carried away by her temper, she'd later say, "That wasn't his way. . . . It's a good thing he loves us." And we knew she *knew* his love. This lady said so many novenas and rosaries a day I never did get the count straight. Nor did I ever even try to say as many. Nor did she try to make me. If the proof of the pudding is in the eating, her prayers and praying were authentic. We just had to reflect on how she treated us to know that!

That's one way to be prayerful. What is your prayerful person's way?

More importantly, what does "praying" mean for you, in your life, in your present circumstances? How do you go about praying? What happens? What might that mean?

Suppose you answer those questions for yourself. More likely than not, your answers will engender other questions. How do you test out your answers? Not in a way that is "right" or "wrong," because there's no "right" or "wrong" way to pray, but for validation, further insight, and perhaps challenge.

For Christians the best model is Jesus. If we go through the Gospels and notice when he prayed, we find a large variety of times and places. He "went apart" into the hills or desert, so sometimes he prayed alone. He prayed with his disciples; he prayed with friends, in crowds, and in the temple. He prayed when he was afraid (Gethsemane); hopeful (Last Supper); sad (Lazarus); filled with pity (widow of Naim); in pain (Crucifixion); before decisions (choosing his apostles); happy (when the apostles came back from their preaching). What might that realization mean for us?

For me it means that any time, any place, any circumstance is appropriate for prayer. Any mood, any situation, is appropriate for prayer. How conscious of this am I during my days?

There's a saying commonly found on banners and posters: "Prayer changes things." I'm inclined to say it differently: "Prayer changes me." Prayer isn't a matter of getting what I want from God, as if he were some super Santa Claus. It's more a matter of getting to be, day by day, more fully the kind of person I ultimately want to be.

St. Thomas calls prayer "unveiling our desires before God." Prayer shows me to myself in my act of revealing myself to my God. That revelation, in turn, can show me where I need to change. A director can help me with this. I need to face, accept, and even enjoy my limitations. They are part of my reality. I need to explore: my guilt, which may be real or may be self-punishing, for whatever reason; my doubts, which may be legitimate or may be allowed to immobilize me; my anxieties, which can lead to productive action or may use up my energy; my resistances, which allow me to avoid confronting some of my behaviors and impulses. What did I learn from the Island phantasy? Or the Two Boats? I need very much to pay attention consciously to how I feel about myself. (Think back to the Wise Person or the Tomorrow phantasy.) *Self–esteem* and *self–concept* are the words commonly used. Yet esteem for oneself is very important. Many good people tend to brush it off as unimportant, as if it is "proud" to think about it. Still self–acceptance needs reflection. Not a casual, offhand, "Of course I accept myself." What is needed is a correct assessment of myself, done with neither bravado nor apology. Then behaviors that are congruent with this assessment can follow.

That is one way the phantasies given can serve us. They are one way to help ourselves identify our emotional attitudes and judgments. While spiritual direction is centered on our relationship with God, it is concerned with the whole person. When we as whole persons want to love the Lord God with all that we are and all that we have, we have to *know* all that we are and have as human beings. When there is diffidence, when masks are habitual, when defenses are up, then tools like the phantasies can be useful in cutting through the muddle.

One of the things which constantly intrigues me about us human beings is how connected up we are—how everything about us influences and is influenced by everything else. Look at the ways we come to know ourselves: through reflection, feedback, challenge, comfort with prayer. Look at how important it is to know ourselves to be loving—and forgiving—persons. Again, let's look at prayer for a moment.

Suppose I'm praying the Lord's prayer. Suddenly one of the ending sentences catches me: "Forgive us our trespasses *as we forgive those who. . . .*" Oops! "AS." Dangerous word. How do I forgive? If I am specific (and that is really necessary), how do I forgive the nasty crack about my daughter that I overheard in the beauty parlor the other day? How do I forgive the "rumor" that was carefully planted in my boss's ear? How do I forgive that blatant interference with my spouse? How do I forgive my Dad's being fired, when I *know* the real reason? How do I forgive. . . . You can fill in your own hurts, injustices, worries.

Well, how do you forgive? How do you go about forgiving? That's a serious question and one not frequently asked.

Perhaps it should be prefaced by "Do you *want* to forgive?" I suspect that most of us, down deep, want to. But at the moment, in the heat of the anger or hurt or resentment, we may not. (Try the Relationship phantasy when you are hurting badly.) Do you want to forgive? Why not spend a few minutes paying attention to both why and why not to determine where you are on the issue. I want to forgive for *my* sake. I need to "give for" (forgive) the offending person because that offense put my life a bit (or a great deal) out of balance. To restore the balance, I forgive. In forgiving, I am better.

How do we go about forgiving? People give many answers to that question. Sometimes we start talking to a friend (but, if it is a mutual friend, not asking the friend to choose sides). Sometimes we begin by praying about it. Sometimes we go directly to the person and talk it through (a good method, especially if the other person cooperates; that cooperation, however, is not always forthcoming). Another method involves trying to understand where the other person is coming from, what pressures are being suffered; or perhaps by reflecting on Jesus' words: "Father forgive them, they know not what they do." (Often enough all of us are unaware of the impact of our behavior on others; we are so engrossed in what we mean.) Another way is simply to find some way to let go of the anger. The list could go on indefinitely.

How do you know when you have forgiven the person? Think about it. How do you know? People have told me that they know when they aren't preoccupied with the person or offense anymore; when they stop phantasizing vengeance (often of the most dire sort); when they meet the offender and they don't get a knotted stomach, a tight chest, or an impulse to turn and to go in the other direction. How do *you* know?

During the process of forgiving, what do you learn about yourself? Whether it is talking to a friend, praying, reflecting, or working it through with the other person, there almost certainly is some learning for ourselves.

Somewhere in the process (if I am loving my neighbor *as* myself), there is also forgiving my neighbor *as* myself. Somehow, there is an aspect of self–forgiveness. Generally I find some relationship to the first commandment, too. "I am the Lord your God. You shall not have strange gods before me."

When I was younger I didn't pay much attention to that commandment. After all, I am not a pagan! Now I pay a great deal of attention to that commandment. I still am not a pagan. However, I keep finding strange gods in my life. If truly I believe there is *one* God, why do I expect everyone to be perfect? To treat me perfectly well all of the time? Why do I expect of myself no failures? Perhaps I need to better learn that there truly is but one God. My neighbor is not the one God. No more than I am. Perhaps, in my act of forgiving, I learn better what it means to be creature. Perhaps I learn again that the human condition is rather messy and that compassion for myself and for others is an everyday Christian affair. (How did you experience the Farewell phantasy? Or the Toys phantasy?)

While I'm in the process of forgiving, I learn I can't do it right away and by myself. I need to call on the help of the Lord. When the wound is deep, I am not generous or simple enough to acknowledge it and let it go. Many times the best I can do is to ask for help to acknowledge it honestly ("Yes, I was hurt") and to let it go, with compassion for both of us. It may take days, weeks, months, years. It may be a very good reminder to me to keep asking for help in forgiving, and a good reminder of my creaturely limitations.

How good am I at forgiving myself? Not with arrogance, not casually, but with truth and love? With simplicity, saying (and meaning), "I did it" (or "I didn't do it"). "It was wrong. I am sorry." Then integrating the experience into my life and moving on securely in the mercy and love of God.

There's yet another hard aspect to the bundle of forgiveness. How do I accept forgiveness? When I have been the offender, how do I ask for, and accept, forgiveness? If I consciously experience in my own life how long it takes me to forgive another, what is my stance toward one whom I have offended? It may take that other person a long time and much struggle to be able to forgive me. In a deep sense, how do I help that person to forgive me?

It doesn't do me much good to spend hours and hours in quiet prayer if I nurse hurts and vengeance. Solitude and silence don't do much for my everyday living if I am not at peace with others. I need to be a forgiving person: giving forgiveness, receiving forgiveness.

Prayer, you see, isn't always a pleasant experience. Who would have thought that a simple "Our Father" might have "bit" so deeply into my soul that I was constrained to take the time to reflect on who I want to forgive? Why? How do I go about forgiving? How do I know when I have forgiven? And . . . what are my expectations?

My expectations must be of myself. I have no right, nor do I have the power, to make others change to suit me. I change. I become more compassionate, more accepting, more conscious of human conditions, more aware of what it means for all of us to be creatures. I become more tranquil. I become more prayerful. Or I don't. I need to face that, too.

It isn't easy. As my integrity deepens, I am liberated from my preoccupation with myself. I am better able to love others *as* myself, to forgive them *as* myself. I am better able to love and forgive myself, and to depend on the help of God, my friends, and my own effort.

Prayer may show me my nasty side, my self–righteousness in my lack of forgiving. It might also make me more aware of how much I justify and defend myself. Listen to how I tell God how right I am! Or reflections on a Scripture text might bring to the surface how hard I work at pleasing others, or how I do the right thing rather superficially. Prayer (when I get around to it), and the excuses I make to the Lord about why I haven't attended to him lately, may say things to me about my busyness and what I have let happen to me in my ministry; about how shallow, how unreflective I'm becoming. Why do I let those things happen to me? I always have some excuse. Often I cannot isolate the real cause by myself. (Excuses are easy.) A director may better enable me to see myself and to make (if I so choose) better decisions, which will bring what I say I believe and how I live into harmony. (It's usually a good thing when a director can say something like, "Remember your God Tree phantasy? And the Child

123

under the Tree? How might those fit in with what you are saying now?")

Perhaps your life is already well–integrated. Perhaps the way you live, and what you say you believe, and the way you pray, are pretty much of a whole. Your prayer is faithful. Now what?

Usually things don't stay still for long. We all know that. Look at how quickly spring comes and goes! How short a time we have apple and cherry blossoms. What was it Jesus said about those who have been given much? The demands are many. If not in quantity, then in quality. As intimacy with God deepens, and life becomes more simple, I think it is even more important to have companionship in prayer. We need help in discerning if what we are experiencing is of God, or wishful thinking, or some illusion. Is our inner security complacency or the inner peace which accompanies life in the Spirit?

A touchstone of discernment, of course, is found in Gal. 5:22–23, where the fruits of the Spirit are listed. In the long run I know how I am or how another person is, by the way we behave. To know how we behave—beyond our intentions to the way other people experience us—we need help. (How did you treat the obstacles to the Cave or the Storekeeper?) People can give us feedback. Feedback can be inconsistent, contrary, contradictory. It's too facile to say to another, "That's your problem," and drop it. It might be the other person's problem. We might not be the cause, but the target of the other one's anger. Then again, it might be our doing, at least partially. We need someone to help keep us honest in responding to others. In that, too, we have the example of Jesus. Luke tells us that Jesus asked, "Who do men say I am?" The apostles found an easy out: "Some say . . . Some say. . . ." Jesus pressed them, "Who do YOU say I am?" And for once, Peter didn't have his foot in his mouth. We, too, need to ask, "Who do people say I am?" We need to listen.

Jesus came to bring us life to the fullest. A while back I asked, "What does that mean to us?" Now I am ready for a partial answer.

As I pray, as I forgive and accept forgiveness, as I am

increasingly aware of myself, of my attitudes, and my impact on other people, I am better able to acknowledge the truth of how I am, of how I want to be, and to take steps to allow that to happen. When I push the things I don't like about myself down and out of sight, I have to use energy to keep them there. It's like being in a pool with a big beach ball. Am I physically able to hold the ball under water? Sure! Do I do much else? Not really. And what happens when I let go of the ball? Well, that's rather what it is like when I hold down, out of my sight, those aspects of my behavior, memories, and impulses that I find unacceptable. It takes enormous energy. A toll on my relationships. When I am aware that I am doing that, when I have the courage (maybe with the help of a friend, a director) to look at those things and decide what to do about them (other than hiding them), then I have all that energy to use for living. "I have come to bring life and life to the fullest." My energy is no longer wasted holding down beach balls—or embarrassing memories.

It's a lifelong process, this growing toward God, this becoming free—and holy. At different life stages it takes different modes of expression.

In directing other people (as well as in reflecting on one's own prayer), it's a useful thing for the director to be aware of chronological age and adult stages of development. Just as you can't put a pencil into the hand of a nine–month–old child and teach the baby to write, so too are different abilities present in adults at different ages. What marriage or religious vows mean and require at twenty–five, for instance, may not be precisely what they mean and require at forty–five or at seventy–five. Yet they are the same sacred promises. Each age has its own joys and its sacrifices, its own way of living the promises. In addition to attending to adult developmental stages, the directee's "age" in faith development also is very important. There's a big difference between a person who has had a waving "hello" relationship with God on most Sundays, and another who has had a rather steady awareness of his providence in daily life. There's a difference between one in whom the yearning for God has been growing steadily, and one who has undergone a sudden conversion experience.

Directors need to be sensitive to the faith history and present faith of the directee.

There is more. Directors are, to a noticeable extent, paying more heed to the personality of the directee. The directee's characteristics (quiet, party–goer, outgoing, receptive, reasonable, plodding, intuitive, klutzy, fun–loving, organized, scattered, muddling along, well–planned) will have an influence on his or her prayer style, since prayer is part of the person's life. If prayer can occur at any time, in any place, under any circumstances, and during any mood, then a person's prayer style simply has to relate to the way that person is. It will not be an ill–advised imitation of some admired saint—or even of the person you named earlier as a model praying person.

Suggestions made to directees cannot be handed out like most clothing—ready–made and off the rack. There simply are too many variables of person and of experience that require notice and respect. Besides, since the real director is the Holy Spirit, what happens is generally a surprise of some sort—unexpectable and so right!

I remember one of the first directed retreats I gave. The most useless thing I did was to prepare Scripture for the person before he appeared. The smartest thing I did was to spend quiet time consciously in God's presence before the man came. Certainly I knew where the man was in his prayer—the day before. Each morning, when he spoke of the time since our last meeting, he spoke of the surprising things which had happened to him in his prayer. Some days he moved so fast it was a bit hard to keep up with the Spirit! We experience over and over, how such growth is the work of the Spirit, far beyond our own power or expectations.

So, in the course of the director–directee relationship, nothing human and nothing of God is excluded. Meetings are not problem–centered in the sense that therapy sessions are, although problems are not neglected since they need to be incorporated into the life of the person. Relationship with God and with neighbor cannot be compartmentalized away from the rest of life. Each of us is *one* person. Our ongoing integration within ourselves and with our life circumstances is essential to living "life to the fullest." (What did the Store phantasy show you? How did the Wise Person affect you?)

A while back I said that, traditionally, spiritual direction is one–to–one: director and directee. Most of the time that is the situation. It has all the advantages of full personal attention, confidentiality, and the relative ease of saying difficult things, perhaps for the first time, to an audience of one.

Still, I'd like to propose an alternative. It seems to me that there are distinct advantages (and some risks) in an alternate model.

The idea came to me after I became acquainted with Dr. Donald J. Tyrell, a clinical psychologist in private practice in Arlington Heights, a Chicago suburb. Over the past years Dr. Tyrell has developed a method of "individual therapy in a group setting." It is his contention, borne out by more than twenty years of practice, that people are helped more rapidly, with less investment in time and money and with more resources at their disposal, in a group setting. It requires—insofar as is humanly possible—that each person be both intellectually and affectively as honest as possible. People are encouraged to be generous with their experience, insofar as it might be helpful to the member of the group who has the floor. While the therapist (analogously, the director) is presumed to have requisite knowledge and skills, no one can have all the experience that is present in a group. Besides, in one–on–one counseling, the counselee is always "on stage." In individual work in a group setting, there is a natural ebb and flow of tension and attention for any one person. While attending to another person, insights into one's own dilemma or problem surface. Although the requirements are demanding, the results are generally very satisfying.

It occurred to me that this way of approaching situations is so productive in therapy, why might it not be productive in spiritual direction? Isn't it a valid and fair assumption that people are serious about their spiritual growth? The hunger I see says yes. Will not serious Christians allow themselves to be vulnerable, to receive and to offer companionship on the spiritual journey, just as people do in their emotional education? The hunger I see says yes. Might not the expected benefit of more development, with more resources, and in a shorter time be expected? I think so. Might not more consistent honesty be expected, a "not missing what's really going on," when six or eight people are attending instead of just one? I think so.

At least, that's my experience with people who come for individual spiritual direction in a group setting. Men and women, ordained and not, all Christian (not all Roman Catholic) are in the group which meets biweekly for two hours, serving our needs in this area.

We have a ritual of sorts. First we go around the room. Each person speaks as desired about the past two weeks and indicates what—if anything—will be presented to the group for attention.

That process gives the director a sense of timing. It doesn't mean "speak now or forever hold your peace." If an issue is triggered off in a person later in the session, there's freedom to raise it. Toward the end of the session we go around the room again. Each person says how the time was experienced, what it meant. If something else has occurred to a person, there is this additional chance to present it.

Such a group takes form slowly. Limits are tested; so is trustworthiness. Sacred things are at stake and people rightfully proceed with care. Besides, while people generally are intellectually honest, emotional honesty is a rarer commodity. Gradually the women and men in the group become aware of each other's rationalizing, evasion, and excusing, and begin to confront these behaviors.

In spiritual direction groups I will not permit a "hot seat" technique. Confrontation is had with care to allow maximum freedom. To my way of thinking a challenge can be made in a way that leaves the person free to face it without provoking self–protective or defensive behaviors. There's nothing demeaning or humiliating in this process. Quite to the contrary, it is freeing to the person engaging in it.

"How can this be?" you might be asking.

Well, I think it's because most of us are basically truthful and quite good. When we are free from needing to make an impression, look good, fulfill someone's expectations (or our own), or protect ourselves, then we are more ready to look at ourselves: AS IS. When a number of people look at themselves, and each other, AS IS, and know AS IS is quite enough, then I see (and I experience) good things happening. We want to be better. Here's a safe place, a safe group, to expose the obstacles. Here's a safe place, a safe group, to expose our goodness—and have it taken seriously. Then we are truly free to choose to move on.

A variety of factors brings about this situation but basically it is the goodness and willingness of people. Depending on how the discussion goes, we may or may not use phantasies. They are one of the useful means we use.

I find the emerging community we experience a verification of the Gospel's "See how these Christians love one another." We do. And I am grateful to all of us for the reality of it.

For you who read this book I wish similar struggle and similar joy. I wish you the experience of other believers among whom each of you can be who you are called to be: the people of God, living life to the fullest.

 Notes

Notes

Additional books for personal growth and spiritual development

Avoiding Burnout: Time Management for D.R.E.s

Just as the title suggests, this helpful new book gives sound advice on organizing and correcting those areas that overwork and overload the person who directs educational programs for a parish. Written by Clarice Flagel. (Order #1782, $4.95)

Mending Our Nets

Here is everything that is needed to establish and manage a parish high school religious education program. Included in this 148-page how-to book are dozens of checklists, worksheets, guidelines, flowcharts, and resource lists. Created by Rosemary Torrence and commissioned by the Religious Education Office, Diocese of Cleveland. (Order #1757, $7.95)

Program Materials for "Imagine That"

For information regarding a video tape program available for use with this book contact Wm. C. Brown Company Publishers.

R.C.I.A.: Foundations of Christian Initiation

Providing a general introduction to Christian initiation as well as guidelines and starters for beginning the implementation of initiation is the focus of this new book. Commissioned by the Archdiocese of Dubuque, Office of Religious Education. (Order #1781, $7.95)

R.C.I.A.: A Practical Approach to Christian Initiation

This 136-page book offers a complete guide for implementing the Rite of Christian Initiation of Adults. Written by a ministry team headed by Sr. Rosalie Curtin. (Order #1759, $7.95)

To order, send your name and address and the titles and order numbers of the books you want. Please include 50¢ for postage and handling. Payment must accompany order. Send to:

WM. C. BROWN COMPANY PUBLISHERS
Religious Education Division
P.O. Box 539; 2460 Kerper Blvd.
Dubuque, IA 52001